Get **more** out of libraries

Please return or renew this item by the last date shown.

You can renew online at www.hants.gov.uk/library

Or by phoning   0845 603 5631

Hampshire
County Council

Animal
Series editor: Jonathan Burt

Owl

Desmond Morris

REAKTION BOOKS

Published by
REAKTION BOOKS LTD
33 Great Sutton Street
London EC1V ODX, UK
www.reaktionbooks.co.uk

First published 2009

Printed and bound in China

British Library Cataloguing in Publication Data
Morris, Desmond.
    Owl. – (Animal)
    1. Owls.
    2. Owls in literature.
    3. Owls in art.
    I. Title II. Series
    598.9'7-DC22

ISBN: 978 1 86189 525 7

Contents

Introduction

The owl is a contradiction. It is the best known of birds and the least known of birds. Ask anyone, even a small child, to draw an owl and they will do so without hesitation. Ask them when they last saw an owl and they will pause, think hard and then say they can't remember. As a picture in a book – yes; as a bird in a TV documentary – probably; as a cage inmate in a zoo – possibly. But when did they last see a live owl in the wild, in its natural state? That is a different matter.

How has this contradiction arisen? It is easy enough to understand why we so rarely encounter a live owl, for it is a shy night predator with silent flight. Unless we went out of our way to spot one and made organized nocturnal forays with special equipment, we would have little chance of coming face to face with one. It is harder to understand why we are so familiar with its appearance, if we see so little of it. The answer lies in its unique head shape. Like human beings the owl has a wide, rounded head, with a flat face and a pair of large, wide-set, staring eyes. This gives it an unusually human quality that no other bird can match and in ancient times it was sometimes referred to as the human-headed bird. We call ourselves *Homo sapiens*, meaning 'wise man' and because the owl has a human-looking head we refer to it as a 'wise old bird'. In reality an owl is not as wise as a crow or a parrot, but we think of it as wise simply because of its superficial resemblance to us.

The White Owl, a portrait of the barn owl by Eleazar Albin in 1731. The iconic shape of the owl has been a joy for illustrators for centuries.

A child's-eye view: *Wise Owl, Sad Owl, Angry Owl* by Matilda, age 10, ink and pencil on paper, 2008.

It is this humanoid stare that makes us feel we know the owl. And it is the broad head and the big, forward-facing eyes that make it impossible for us to look at an owl and not feel that we are in the presence of a deep-thinking avian relative. This makes us, at the same time, rather sentimental about owls and rather scared of them. If they are so wise and yet they only come out at dead of night, perhaps they are up to no good? Like burglars they stalk their prey when their victims are at their most vulnerable. Like vampires they only draw blood when the sun has gone down. Perhaps, instead of wisdom, there might be something evil about the owl?

When we examine the history of our relationship with owls we find that it has, indeed, frequently been a symbol of both wisdom and evil. Wise or wicked, wicked or wise, the image of the owl keeps altering. For several thousand years these two iconic values have kept swapping and changing. Another of the contradictory qualities of the much misunderstood owl.

In this book I want to examine both these roles, and others too. For the evil owl can suddenly change into a protective owl if its imagined violence can be harnessed and turned against our enemies. In India it has also been seen as a vehicle for a goddess, swooping down from the sky, and in Europe, by some, as a symbol of obstinacy and by others as an emblem of calm in the face of extreme provocation. In the twenty-first century, when we are at last coming to appreciate the wild fauna of our planet and worry about its dramatic decline, we are also keen to understand the fascinating biology of the owl.

So there are many owls to be examined here: the wise owl, the evil owl, the protective owl, the transporting owl, the obstinate owl, the calm owl and the natural owl. And there have been many different epochs and cultures in which our interest in owls has led to a fascinating collection of myths, legends and artefacts, all dominated by the owls' hypnotic stare.

On a personal note, from my days as a zoo curator I have known many captive owls, and during the days when I was

A Bestiary Owl,
12th century.

9

travelling around making television programmes about animal life, I met many more. But if I am honest, I have – like you, I suspect – met very few owls in the wild, in their natural habitats. There was, however, one memorable encounter that I still recall vividly in every detail, even though it took place over sixty years ago, when I was at boarding school. I had wandered off into the countryside near the school one summer's afternoon, and saw something strange in the corner of a field. I approached slowly and silently because I could see that it was some kind of bird, standing immobile on the ground. As I drew closer, it still did not move. Then, when I was about ten feet away from it, I realized with a sudden jolt of recognition that it was a blood-covered, severely injured owl. It must have been shot, caught up in a trap, entangled in some sort of sharp wiring, or hit by a car in the night. Its injuries were horrific and it was clearly dying slowly and in great pain. It was beyond veterinary help. What was I to do?

As there was no hope of saving it, my choice of action was deeply unpleasant. The easy option was to leave it alone, but this would mean that I was condemning it to die in agony. On the other hand, if I killed it, I would be putting it out of its misery, but this would require me to perform a violent act against a helpless victim and to destroy a magnificent bird. As a small schoolboy I found it hard to choose. I looked at the owl and the owl looked at me, its large black eyes registering no emotion. It must have been there for hours, waiting to die, and as we stared at one another I felt a huge emotional attachment to it and a burning anger towards the humans who, directly or indirectly, had caused its wounds.

The year was 1942 and World War II was raging across Europe. Somehow, this blood-splattered owl standing in the corner of a sunlit Wiltshire field seemed to symbolize all the countless humans who would, inevitably, be wounded on that day across a whole continent. How I hated the human species at that moment. I decided I could not take the easy option. I found a large stone, struck the owl on the head with it and killed it. I had ended its suffering but I felt terrible. And to this day I still feel terrible about that moment whenever I think of it. Irrationally, I don't think I would have been so upset if the bird had been a wounded pheasant. And therein lies the power of the owl. We know it is not human, but its human-shaped head sends out signals to our brain that make us identify more closely with it that with pointy-faced birds. As babies we humans respond strongly to a pair of maternal eyes staring down at us. We are genetically programmed to respond in this way and cannot help ourselves. So the owl triggers off a special reaction in us whenever we look at it and this gives us a sense of closeness to it, even though, in truth, it is a complete stranger.

Perhaps the reason why I have decided to write this book is to try and make amends for the damage that had been done to that wounded owl. I want to atone by doing something for owls in general, explaining how fascinating they are biologically, and how rich and varied is their symbolism and their mythology. On the pages that follow I will do my best for them . . .

1 Prehistoric Owls

We know from fossil remains that owls have existed as a distinct lineage for at least 60 million years. This makes them one of the oldest known groups of birds and gives them plenty of time to have refined their highly specialized way of life as nocturnal predators.

It is only during the very last part of their long reign that they will have encountered that irritatingly intrusive species, the human being. Happily for them, this encounter will have been far less damaging than for many other kinds of birds. They have rarely been put into tiny cages like so many songbirds or hunted for the table like countless game birds. But like all wild birds they have suffered the indignity of seeing their habitats destroyed over vast areas of land, their woodlands and forests decimated and their prey poisoned by pest-controllers. Despite these depredations they still thrive all over the world and, apart from the polar wastes, there are very few land regions where they are absent.

The very first evidence of man's knowledge of the existence of owls can be dated at about 30,000 years ago. The discovery of this evidence is very recent. On 18 December 1994 three cave-explorers found a hidden entrance in an underground cavern in south-east France. Dragging away the rubble that blocked this entrance they unearthed a narrow passageway. Squeezing through it they found themselves in a vast cave, its walls covered with beautiful prehistoric paintings. There were all the usual animals we know so well from cave art: bison, deer, horses, rhinos, mammoths and other large mammals, but what was so surprising about this newly discovered cave was that, deep inside, they also came across the incised image of an owl.

This is the oldest representation of an owl known to us at the present time. It depicts a bird with a large, broad, rounded head from which protrude two upright ear-tufts. The eyes are present but rather smudged and there is a strong beak. Below the head the wings are clearly shown with about a dozen vertical lines suggesting plumage. The height of the figure is about 33 cm (13 inches) and its details appear as white lines incised into the yellow ochre colour of the cave wall. The incisions may have been made by a heavy fingernail, but much more likely by a simple stick or tool of some kind.

By a lucky chance the antiquity of this image has been proved by its position in the cave. In the centre of the chamber in which it exists, called the Hillaire Chamber, there is a large crater – a great hole in the ground that subsided in antiquity. The owl image was incised on an overhang above this hole at a spot that is now impossible for a human hand to reach. The hole is 4.5 m (15 feet) deep and the crater has a diameter of 6 m (20 feet). The collapse of the cave floor has conveniently left the owl high and dry, proving beyond any doubt that it is not a modern fake.

This first owl image has been enthusiastically identified as representing a great horned owl. There is no way of confirming this, except to point out that it does have horns and it does appear alongside images of Ice Age mammals such as mammoths, suggesting that it would have to be a very large bird to survive the cold. So, calling it a great horned owl is perhaps not too fanciful a suggestion. A second claim is, however, rather more doubtful. This argues that the prehistoric artists were such good observers that they had noticed that the owl can rotate its head through a wide angle and that the image is meant to show the bird from the rear, with its head twisted to survey whatever was immediately behind it. The reason for this claim is that the wings are supposed to be depicted from the back. This may be so, but it is far more likely that, as with any child drawing an owl, the wings are shown like this, even when viewing the bird from the front, as a simple way of emphasizing that this is a feathered creature.

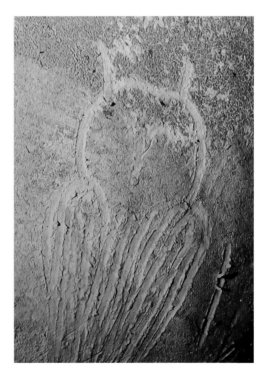

A great horned owl: 30,000-year-old engraved white lines on the roof of a cave at Chauvet, France.

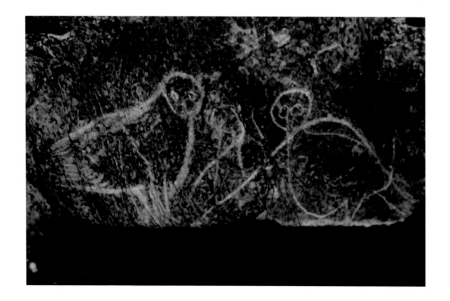

Regardless of these minor quibbles, this unique bird in what is now known as the Chauvet Cave, after its discoverer, provides us with a magnificent beginning to the long love affair that has existed between the human artist and the iconic shape of the owl.[1]

A family of snowy owls: Aurignacian-period art incised in white lines on the roof of Les Trois-Frères Cave in the French Pyrenees.

To find the next owl images we have to move to the southwest of France, to the foothills of the Pyrenees and to a painted cave called the Trois-Frères. This cave is named for three brothers, the sons of Comte Bégouën, who discovered it in 1910. Here, among wall paintings dating from thousands of years later than those in the Chauvet cave, we find not one but three owls. They appear to form a family group with two adults, one on either side of an owl chick. They have been identified as a family of snowy owls, presumably because they co-exist on the walls of this cave with images of a variety of Ice Age animals. If this identification is correct, it means that this species occurred much farther south than it does today, which is not surprising when one considers the dramatic change in climate.[2]

About thirty miles to the east of Trois-Frères, also in the foothills of the Pyrenees, is the little known painted cave of Le Portel. In Gallery One, not far from the entrance, is the image of a bird that has been identified as an owl, in simple black outline, near to that of a horse and a bison.[3] As in the Chauvet Cave, it is a solitary image among numerous horses, deer, bulls and bison. There is also a supposed owl image on the wall of the cave of La Viña in northern Spain and there are three Old Stone Age examples of owl figures in the round, two from Dolní Věstonice in the Czech Republic, fashioned from clay and bone ash, and one from Mas D'Azil in the French Pyrenees, carved from an animal tooth.[4] And that is about the sum total of Palaeolithic owl images.

The most frustrating feature of this small handful of early artefacts is that we have no way of telling how they were viewed by the prehistoric artists who made them. Their very rarity makes the problem even more diffcult to solve. There are, by comparison, literally hundreds of bison, deer, horses and other

Palaeolithic owl images redrawn (*left to right*): a painted owl silhouette from Le Portel Cave, France; two owl figurines from Dolní Vestonice in the Czech Republic; an owl carved from an animal tooth, from Mas D'Azil in the French Pyrenees.

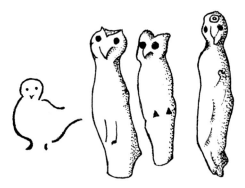

large prey species on the cave walls of France. It is obvious enough why the early artists were so fascinated by those animals. They provided the meat that enabled the small human tribes to survive in the freezing climate of the day. But why owls? Were they an occasional addition to the primeval diet, or did they possess some symbolic role, the nature of which we will never know? If we are to understand owl symbolism, we have to move on to much later depictions of these birds, from eras when we do have some idea about local beliefs and superstitions.

2 Ancient Owls

The ancient civilizations of the Middle East and Southern Europe provide us with some memorable owls.

About four thousand years ago in Babylonia (now in southern Iraq) an artist fashioned a strange clay relief plaque in the centre of which stands a fearsome naked goddess of human form, but with the wings and feet of an owl. To indicate her power she is depicted treading on two scrawny lions. She is flanked by a pair of large owls, standing stiffly erect and facing forward, giving the impression that they are her guardian companions or familiars.

This unique work of art, once believed to be a fake but now proved to be genuine, shows us a goddess whose name is unknown, but who has been variously identified as Babylonian Ishtar, Babylonian Lileth, Caananite Anat, Sumerian Inanna, or perhaps Ereshkigal, Inanna's sister and Queen of the Underworld. Because of this scholarly confusion, its new owners, the British Museum, refer to her simply as the Queen of the Night. Whoever she is, she appears to be the first of the many forms of the Owl Goddess. At this stage she seems to be a thoroughly aggressive, predatory creature, whose massive talons could subdue almost any enemy, but in later incarnations, such as the Greek Athene, her bellicose nature, although still present, is restrained by the acquisition of wisdom.

Although it is possible to find some exquisite examples of painted owls or owls carved in relief on the tomb walls and buildings of ancient Egypt, there is surprisingly no Egyptian Owl God, or even a name for the owl in the ancient Egyptian language. In hieroglyph writing, the owl-glyph has the sole function of providing the sound or letter *m*. There are two interesting features of this glyph. All other birds and, indeed, all other forms of animal life, are shown in profile when rendered as hieroglyphs. This is a rigid tradition that is only abandoned with the owl, whose body is shown in profile, but whose head is turned through 90 degrees to face the viewer head-on. This was presumably the only way that the hieroglyph writer could make it absolutely clear that an owl, rather than some other bird of prey, was being depicted. A second curious feature of owl glyphs is that the birds are sometimes shown with their legs broken, as if there has been an attempt to make it impossible for the birds to come to life and launch an attack.

Although the owl did not play the prominent role in Egyptian religion that we see for the falcon, the ibis or the vulture, we do know that it was sufficiently respected to have been accorded the honour of occasionally being mummified. Several different species have been identified from mummified remains, including the barn owl.

It has been suggested that the owl may have been associated in a strange way with the human soul. The Egyptians envisaged

'The Queen of the Night' (the 'Burney Plaque'), terracotta plaque of baked straw-tempered clay, Mesopotamian 1800–1750 BC. Probably from Babylonia (southern Iraq).

Hieroglyph of an owl, a painting on the outer coffin of Djehuty-nekht, a prince of the Middle Kingdom; 12th Dynasty Egypt, 1991–1876 BC.

An owl hieroglyph drawing of the Ramesside period, c. 1305–1080 BC.

the soul having separate parts. There was the *ka*, concerned with creative, life-giving energy – the life force. After death, the *ka* resided in the tomb, where it required sustenance in the form of offerings.[1] There was also the *ba*, the non-physical ghost of the person; and the *akh*, which was the eternal spirit that lived on in the afterlife and was the result of the *ka* and *ba* combining. For this combination to occur the *ba* had to travel to join the *ka* and, in order for the physical body of the deceased to survive the afterlife, the *ba* had to return to the tomb every evening. It was believed to have undertaken this nightly journey in the form of a human-headed bird. It has been pointed out that this human-headed bird 'may have derived from the owls that frequented the tombs'.[2] It is easy to understand how the eerie, half-glimpsed owl, with its human-shaped head, flitting around near a tomb at dusk, could have given rise to this idea of a bird-like embodiment of the *ba*.

GREECE

Among the ancient civilizations, it was in Athenian Greece that the owl reached the zenith of its appreciation as a symbolic bird. It was here that wisdom and the owl became synonymous. Athens had been named after its protecting goddess, Athene or Athena, and the owl was sacred to her. For hundreds of years, from the sixth to the first centuries BC, Athenian coins were minted with the image of the goddess on one side and the owl on the other. It was this coin that introduced the concept of 'heads or tails' that became popular on many later coins. These Greek coins were known colloquially as 'owls', and in his play *The Birds* (414 BC) Aristophanes jokes that silver owls are the best kind because they 'will never leave you; they will dwell in your home and nest in your purse, hatching out small change'.

Owl of Athene, a Greek tetradrachm from Athens, 109–108 BC.

The Owl of Athene, Goddess of Wisdom, on a modern Greek 1 euro coin.

The bird that was the model for the Athenian coin is thought to be the little owl (*Athene noctua*) and it is usually depicted in the Egyptian hieroglyph posture, with its body in profile and its head facing forward. In a few coins it appears instead in a frontal posture with its wings spread.

The best-known Greek coin on which the owl appeared was the tetradrachm, the four drachm silver piece, but it appeared on coins of many denominations, including the decadrachm and the less valuable didrachm, drachm, hemidrachm, tetrobol, diobol, trihemiobol, obol, hemiobol, tritartemorion, trihemitartemorion, tetartemorion and hemiartemorion. (The challenge of working out the change when shopping in the agora must have been daunting.) The drachm was a coinage unit based on weight. One Greek drachm = 4.37 gm. These coins live on, even today, in the form of the modern Greek 1 euro coin, of which the Athenian owl is the centrepiece. In recent years the Athenian owl has also appeared both on Greek banknotes and Greek postage stamps. Its fame spread far and wide, and it is claimed that the American president Theodore Roosevelt used to carry an Athenian owl piece with him as a lucky charm.

The image of the Goddess Athene on an Apulian red-figure *glaux skyphos* (owl cup). A Greek red-and-black glazed ceramic bowl, 4th century BC.

In ancient times the Athenian owl also appeared on many Greek ceramic vessels, especially small measuring cups called *glaux skyphos* (owl cups) of the fourth century BC. It is thought that the presence of an owl image on one of the cups made it an officially recognized measuring device in classical Athens. Significantly, there is in the Louvre a little Greek vessel on which is shown the goddess Athene at war, carrying a spear. The odd feature of this particular image is that here Athene has been transformed almost entirely into the figure of an owl. The only human features that survive are her arms. Here, instead of being Athene's owl, the bird has become the goddess herself.

The reason for this close association between Athene and the owl does not appear to have been accurately recorded by the ancient Greeks themselves, which has allowed for endless academic debate ever since. One suggestion is that Athene had a precursor in the form of the prehistoric Mesopotamian Eye Goddess. She is known to us in the form of small idols that consist of little more than a simple body topped by a huge pair of circular, staring eyes. These idols, dating from 3000 BC, may not have been representative of owls themselves, but their staring eyes may well have led to comparisons with the eyes of owls and, in this way, to have linked Athene to this type of bird. A millennium later, in 2000 BC, small clay figurines of owl-headed goddesses were being made in large numbers in ancient Syria, so Athene may simply have been a late-comer in the long line of owl goddesses in the Middle East.

An alternative view suggests that owls were often seen flying around near the great temple of the goddess, the Parthenon in Athens, and that their presence there may have led to the owl's adoption as the bird sacred to the goddess. In fact, these two rival theories do not really conflict and may, indeed, simply have reinforced one another. Incidentally, owls must have been

unusually common in Athens because there was a proverb about 'taking owls to Athens' that had the same meaning as the British phrase 'taking coals to Newcastle'.

Another, rather ingenious, suggestion relates the owl to the goddess via her menstrual cycles. Briefly expressed, the argument goes like this: The owl is a bird of moonlight. The moon has a monthly cycle. The goddess has a monthly cycle. Therefore the owl and the goddess are intimately linked. When factual records are absent it is wonderful what the human imagination can do when faced with a puzzling question.

Whatever the truth about the original link between the goddess and the owl, there is no doubt that the bird was regarded as a totemic animal by the Athenian Greeks, capable of bringing them good fortune. In his popular play *The Wasps* (422 BC) Aristophanes, for example, mentions the Athenian owl as a good omen in battle, when Athene 'sent her night bird; and as the owlet flew across the host, our armies hope and joyous omens drew. So by the help of Heaven, ere yet the day did close, we shouted victory, and routed all our foes.'

A powerful belief did indeed develop that the appearance of Athene in the shape of an owl was a crucial sign foretelling that Greek forces would triumph in battle. It was taken so seriously that one Greek general used to keep an owl hidden in a cage among his baggage so that he could release it to circle over his troops and give them the courage necessary to ensure victory.[3] 'There goes an owl!' was an Athenian saying meaning 'there are signs of victory'.[4]

In an earlier period the rival Greek city–state of Corinth had also employed the owl as an image for some of its ceramic

A screech owl perfume container, a Proto-Corinthian terracotta vase, 7th century BC.

Ascalaphus turned into an owl: having revealed to Zeus that Persephone has eaten pomegranate seeds (thus ensuring her continued confinement in Hades), in revenge she sprinkles him with transforming Phlegethon water.

vessels and in the Louvre there is a famous seventh-century BC Proto-Corinthian perfume container (*aryballos*) in the form of an owl-shaped vase. It has a curious shape, with the owl's head twisted to one side, as though the Corinthian potter who fashioned it was still under Egyptian influence and was to a degree imitating the hieroglyph owl, with its body in profile and its head turned to face the onlooker.

The owl also figures in the Greek legend of Ascalaphus. He was an Underworld spirit, the son of Acheron and Orphne, who betrayed the fact that Persephone had eaten a pomegranate in the Underworld. She had been told that she could only return to the upper world if she did not eat anything while she was in the Underworld. She was punished for her misdeed and took her revenge on Ascalaphus by turning him into an owl. It is a fair question to ask why being turned into an owl was such a terrible fate when this bird was so revered by the ancient Greeks.

The answer is an intriguing one, namely that Ascalaphus was not turned into just any owl, but specifically into a screech owl. The screech owl was the animal familiar of Hades, the god of the Underworld, and in mythological terms was quite distinct from the revered bird of Athene, which was the little owl. Ovid describes the screech owl as 'a loathsome bird, ill omen for mankind, a skulking screech owl, sorrow's harbinger'.

ROME

In ancient Rome the goddess Athene became transformed into the goddess Minerva. When the Roman armies subdued those of the Greeks they co-opted their guardian figure and, as their Roman goddess Minerva had virtually the same qualities as the Greek Athene, they borrowed her sacred bird and made it their own. Attached to Minerva, however, the owl fared less well because there was already a widespread belief among the Roman populace that owls were evil creatures and symbols of death.

One of the popular Roman superstitions was that witches could turn themselves into owls and swoop down on sleeping babies and suck their blood, a belief that nudged the owl into the world of vampires. If an owl was heard to hoot it meant that a witch was approaching, or that someone would die soon. It was claimed than an owl had hooted just before the deaths of Julius Caesar, Augustus and Agrippa. To see an owl in daylight was thought to be a particularly bad omen and, if an owl could be caught, it would be killed and its body nailed to a door to protect a house from harm. In the first century AD, Columella, in his great work on Roman agriculture, states that owl bodies were hung up by country people specifically to avert storms.

In his great *Natural History* (AD 77), Pliny the Elder says of the owl that 'if he be seen to fly either within cities, or otherwise abroad in any place, it is not for good, but prognosticates some fearful misfortune.' He then records what happened when an owl was observed in the centre of the great city of Rome. The owl entered 'the very secret sanctuary within the Capitol at Rome . . . whereupon . . . the city of Rome that year made general processions to appease the wrath of the gods and was solemnly purged by sacrifices.'[5] Pliny is sceptical about all this and, as a good scientist, records that 'I myself know of cases where owls have sat on houses where no misfortune followed.' Quite so, but perhaps the ancient Romans enjoyed the excitement of their purging sacrifices and all the other protective rituals that they had devised. One thing seems certain, however, and that is that in those far off days there were far more owls settling on houses than we ever see today. The traffic noises and the street lighting have scared them all away.

Some Romans were so convinced that the cry of an owl heralded an imminent death that they would do their utmost to capture the bird and kill it, hoping that this would neutralize the prophecy. Even when the unfortunate bird was dead, there were fears that it would have supernatural powers that would enable it to come to life again, so its body was cremated and its ashes thrown into the River Tiber.

Owls were also thought to be the messengers of sorcerers who danced on the graves of the dead. It is easy to guess how this last belief could have started, because owls often frequent graveyards where, on a moonlit night, they might be seen to swoop down on an unsuspecting mouse, and the act of actually grabbing it could have been interpreted as a sort of dance.

Owls, or parts of them, were used in magical practices. It was believed that if you could place an owl's feather on someone's sleeping body without waking them up, you would be able to discover their secrets. And if you happened to be travelling abroad, a dangerous undertaking in ancient times, and were unfortunate enough to dream of owls, you were about to encounter a disaster of some kind, such as robbery or shipwreck.

CHINA

In China the image of the owl attracted the attention of a great civilization that flourished in the second millennium BC. The artists of the Shang Dynasty (c. 1500–1045 BC) created some of the most elaborate and beautiful bronze figures the world has ever seen. Among them were a number of majestic owls, covered in incised patterns and relief designs of an amazingly complex kind. They are generally dated to around 1200 BC and take the form of delightful little bronze wine containers called *zun*.[6] Sitting firmly on a tripod made up of the two legs and the base of the stiff tail, these owls are thought to have been used during ceremonies of ancestor worship. The staring eyes are huge and the owl's head is topped with double ear-tufts. On the owl's chest is a bull's head emblem in relief and, bizarrely, the wings are formed from a pair of spiral snakes. The back of the owl's body is adorned with a pair of raptor-like birds with savage, curved beaks. The head of the bird is a removeable lid. In the example shown here there is a knob on top of the head that makes it easy to lift. The knob itself is also fashioned in the shape of a small bird with a long pointed beak and a small crest. This little bird seems to be emerging from the owl's crown.

A number of these remarkable owl figures have been excavated from the grave sites of the walled towns of those ancient feudal kingdoms, where the weight of bronze metal employed in their manufacture was clearly an overt display of an affluent society. No records of the period have survived to enable us to interpret with certainty the symbolism of these owls and several

An owl-shaped
bronze *zun* (wine
vessel) of the Late
Shang Period,
c. 1200 BC.

conflicting suggestions have been put forward to explain why they were favoured. The most plausible of these sees the owls placed in the darkness of the tomb to protect the occupants in their journey to the afterlife. With their ability to see in the dark and strike to kill, the owls would be able to detect dangers better than any other life form and deal with them silently and swiftly. They could then fly with the souls of the dead, guiding them safely to the other world. Perhaps the wings shaped like coiled snakes were thought to be able to beat in the darkness and strike down evil spirits with a lethal venom. We will never know for certain, unless new excavations reveal some long lost records of that ancient period.

A millennium or so later, in the Taoist period, the early Chinese viewed the owl not as a wise old friend, but a violent, horrific figure – the evil predatory bird of the night. For some reason it was believed to be a monster and that owlets would pluck out their mother's eyes or would devour her. If Chinese children were born on 'the day of the owl' (the Summer solstice) they were said to have a violent personality, and might even murder their own mother.

It was perhaps the violent personality of the Chinese owl that led to a link with violent storms. In the Taoist religion, Lei-gong, the God of Thunder, was a chimera whose body was part owl and part man. He had the beak, wings and claws of an owl, but the body of a man. It was his duty to punish human beings who were guilty of secret crimes. The Chinese owl was also associated with lightning because it was said to 'brighten the night' and there was an old custom of placing an owl effigy in each corner of the home to protect the building from being struck by lightning.

Fremont Indian rock art: an owl with spread wings at Nine Mile Canyon, Utah, carved between AD 400 and 1350.

An owl with horns among other animals in a panel at Rochester Creek, Utah.

The owl appears frequently in the arts of the ancient Americas, from the ancient rock art of North America to the painted ceramics of Peru. In particular, the Mochica culture that flourished in northern Peru between AD 100 and 800 has left us with a wide variety of appealing owl ceramic vessels. For the Mochica, the owl was an important and complex symbolic presence representing, on the one hand, wisdom and a magical healer and, on the other hand, a warrior involved in ritual decapitation and the spirits of the dead. So, in this case, the eternal contradiction of the owl – the wise and the wicked – existed within the same culture. In its wise role, it was seen as a human figure that became transformed into its animal counterpart during nocturnal rituals when, as a supernatural owl, it could magically see in the dark. In its wicked role it was a lethal warrior in whom a symbolic comparison was drawn between making war and hunting prey.

It is not surprising therefore that, in its ceramic representations it appears in two guises – as itself in an attractive naturalistic

top left: A Mochica gold bead in the shape of an owl's face.

A Mochica culture painted ceramic vessel in the form of an owl. Northern Peru.

form, and as a sinister human wearing an owl mask and a cloak in the form of owl-wings. Sometimes the masked figure is shown holding a large club and sometimes a human head and a knife, for this is the warrior owl, the predator, the killer. In one example the owl carries a man on its wing, interpreted as a sacrificial victim being taken off to the other world following a ritual slaughter.[7]

So, for the great ancient civilizations, the owl already played an important role in myth and legend. From Babylon and Egypt in the Middle East, to Greece and Rome in early Europe, and as far away as China and South America, images of the owl were being laboriously forged, carved and moulded and its name was being indelibly embedded in local folklore. Following on from this it is almost inevitable that, for the deeply superstitious, the body parts of this iconic bird should have been thought to contain magical powers, as we shall see in the next chapter.

3 Medicinal Owls

In earlier centuries, before scientific medical testing was introduced, many animals suffered useless deaths at the hands of
quack doctors who believed that certain parts of the bodies of
these unfortunate creatures would cure assorted human ail-
ments. The owl was no exception and the range of afflictions
that its body parts were supposed to cure beggars belief. Even
William Shakespeare (1564–1616) contributes to this folly. The
infamous witches who cook up a magic brew in the opening
scene of Macbeth cry out:

> Eye of newt, and toe of frog,
> Wool of bat, and tongue of dog,
> Adder's fork, and blind-worm's sting,
> Lizard's leg, and owlet's wing.

Shakespeare's great rival, Ben Jonson (1572–1637), was not going
to be left out. When he wanted a potion concocted, he suggested:

> The screech owl's eggs and the feathers black,
> The blood of the frog and the bone of his back.

A little earlier, in the fifteenth-century compendium of medical
and biological knowledge the *Hortus Sanitatis*, it is recorded

that a treatment for madness included the placing of an owl's ashes on the lunatic's eyes. This attempted cure was doubtless based on the principle that the owl's wise vision could, in this way, be infused into the madman's wildly distorted vision. In India a related belief saw the eating of owls' eggs as a way of improving night vision. Cherokee Indians preferred to bathe their children's eyes with water containing owl feathers, as a way of giving them the ability to stay awake all night.

One of the strangest medical beliefs, and one that lasted for centuries, was that eating the raw eggs of owls would cure a person of drunkenness. In his seventeenth-century *Speculum Mundi* John Swan comments, 'Some say that the egges of an owl broken and put into the cups of a drunkard, or one desirous to follow drinking, will so work with him, that he will suddenly lothe his good liquor and be displeased with drinking.'[1] This belief presumably came into being because the owl is such a studious, solemn-looking bird that it was felt to epitomize sobriety and therefore to lay sobering eggs. The puzzle with all such quack remedies is what kept them going for so long when they had no merit, unless, of course, the power of suggestion was at work. A variation on the owl-eggs-for-curing-drunkards theme saw the eggs administered repeatedly in glasses of wine. At first glance there appears to be a basic flaw in this version of the treatment but then again, perhaps the eggs made the wine taste so vile that even this method eventually worked.

If the drunkard had over-indulged to the point where he also happened to be suffering from gout, he could cure this painful complaint, it was claimed, by plucking all the feathers from an owl's body, salting it for a week, then placing it in a pot, closing the lid and baking it in an oven to mummify it. This mummified owl was then ground down to a fine powder and mixed with boar's grease to make an ointment. If applied to the 'grieved place' on the gout sufferer's body, this ointment would soon make him well again. As someone once said, fortunate is the animal that has no medicinal value.

Boiled owl-fat is also useful, it was said, for ridding the body of sores. And a paralytic human face, massaged with warm owl's blood, or a warm owl's heart, will soon be cured. Owl's blood in oil will get rid of head lice. Dried and pounded owl's crop will cure the colic. Owl's bile will stop bed-wetting. Owl's bone marrow in oil, dropped into the nose, will stop migraines. And so it goes on. It is a wonder that owls were not rendered extinct by all these pointless treatments.

There is more. An even stranger recommendation was that you should kill an owl, pluck out its heart and place it on the left breast of a sleeping woman. In this context the heart would act as a truth drug and would make the woman disclose her darkest secrets. Alternatively, you could take an owl's heart to war with you and it would make you stronger in battle. Or, if you burnt an owl's feet along with the herb plumbago, this would protect you from venomous snake bites. Pliny mentions all these supposed cures in AD 77, but also takes the trouble to dismiss them as monstrous lies.

In England, Yorkshire folk used to make up an owl soup to treat whooping cough. This was based on the idea that if an owl can keep on whooping without suffering any harm, then the special goodness in the owl soup would, by a process of sympathetic magic, take away the sufferer's pain. Elsewhere, owl egg soup, made while the moon is waning, was thought to cure epilepsy. As owls are so calm and composed and usually sit so still it was believed that the frenzied movements of epileptic fits would be stilled by inbibing their essence.

Perhaps the most bizarre of all owl-based medications is one from Germany that says you can avoid being bitten by a mad dog and contracting rabies if you place the heart and right foot of an owl under your left armpit. With this medical gem we have entered the world of *Monty Python*, but this is only the beginning.

It would be possible to fill a whole book with owl cures, all utterly useless but all fervently employed in earlier centuries. Reading them assembled together, as has been done here, makes one grateful for having been born in a scientific era where control tests must be carried out before any medicine can be made availabe to anxious sufferers. We are never more vulnerable to suggestions than when we are sick and in the past this vulnerability has been exploited by quacks and charlatans to an extent that is hard to believe. Owls, too, should be grateful to modern medicine for making their body parts less attractive. We may be cutting down their forests, but at least we have stopped placing bits of them under our armpits.

4 Symbolic Owls

For thousands of years the owl has been viewed as an evil spirit that silently roams the night sky in search of human victims, intent on doing them harm. Its eerie cries have added to this impression and have often labelled it the herald of doom, destruction and death. Because it only comes out at night and even then remains strangely silent, it reminds us of a stealthy criminal, a thief or murderer who lurks in the darkness. As we have already seen, to the ancient Romans the owl's way of life meant that it was viewed as a feared messenger of death. They were not alone in this totally unjustified, gloomy relationship with the harmless, innocent, pest-destroying owl. Many other cultures have felt the same way.

The Bible is full of owl hatred. There are sixteen mentions of owls in the Old Testament, most of them unkind. For a start, the owl is considered to be unclean and must therefore not be eaten. In Deuteronomy 14 is the instruction 'Thou shalt not eat any abominable thing' and the owl comes into this category of abominations. Indeed, in the list of unclean birds the owl is singled out for special treatment: 'And the owl, and the night-hawk, and the cuckoo, and the hawk after his kind. The little owl, the great owl, and the swan . . .'. It is as though the Bible, to make sure that there is no misunderstanding, adds the little owl and the great owl in case some hungry bird-eater might think that there was a loophole and that some kinds of owls were immune and could be served at table.

In Isaiah 13 we find that when Babylon is doomed to remain uninhabited, 'wild beasts of the desert shall lie there; and their houses shall be full of doleful creatures; and owls shall dwell there, and satyrs shall dance there.' A little later, in Isaiah 34, we find the owl once again portrayed as the inevitable occupant of enemy land, land that 'shall become burning pitch'. Once this land has been laid to waste 'the cormorant and the bittern shall possess it; the owl also and the raven shall dwell in it . . . and it shall be a habitation for dragons, and a court for owls . . . the screech owl also shall rest here and find for herself a place of rest. There shall the great owl make her nest, and lay, and hatch, and gather under her shadow . . .'.

These inauspicious beginnings for the Christian owl were to have a lasting effect on its image in the centuries that followed. In thirteenth-century Europe the owl was portrayed, along with

Owl, monkey and goat in The Luttrell Psalter, c. 1340, line drawing.

the goat and the monkey, as one member of a demonic trio. In a fourteenth-century psalter, a book of psalms, hymns and prayers, there is a satirical drawing of a knight out falconing, with the three pagan animals replacing the noble lord, his steed and his bird. The picture shows a monkey with an owl on its gloved fist riding on a goat.

The early bestiaries could not find a good word to say about the owl. In one, the screech owl was described as 'a loathsome bird because its roost is filthy from its droppings, just as the sinner brings all who dwell with him into disrepute through the example of his dishonourable behaviour. It is ... bound by heavy laziness, the same laziness which binds sinners who are inert and idle when it comes to doing good.'[1] The fact that in reality the owl was intensely active during the night 'doing good' for humanity as an efficient destroyer of rodent pests was clearly unknown to the author of these words.

In medieval times certain Christian theologians employed the owl in an unusual way. They argued that, as a nocturnal being, the bird was a symbol of the Jews. This, they said, was because it was the Jews who had preferred the darkness of their own beliefs to the broad daylight of Christianity. The brains behind this kind of medieval anti-semitism were even cunning enough to use the mobbing of an owl as an example of a Jew being attacked by a righteous gathering of enlightened Christians.

In sixteenth-century England our greatest dramatist played his part in keeping alive the owl's bad reputation. In *Macbeth* Shakespeare has Lady Macbeth refer to the shrieking owl as 'the fatal bellman which gives the sternest goodnight'. And in *A Midsummer Night's Dream*, Puck speaks of the screech owl, screeching loud, that 'Puts the wretch that lies in woe, in remembrance of a shroud'. And he continues, 'Now it is the time of night that graves, all gaping wide, every one lets forth his sprite, in the church-way paths to glide', suggesting that, perhaps, the gliding sprites and the graveyard owls were one and the same and that owls, like predatory vampires, inhabited the tombs until the 'witching hour' when they flapped their Dracula-like wings and flew abroad.

In *Henry vi, Part iii* there is a telling line where Shakespeare has the king speak like an ancient Roman: 'The owl shriek'd at thy birth, an evil sign . . .'. In *Julius Caesar* he confirms his knowledge of the role of the owl in Roman legend, when he has Caesar say 'yesterday the bird of night did sit, even at noon-day, upon the market-place, hooting and shrieking', and Caesar concludes that these 'are portentous things'.

The strong association between the owl and death inspired a seventeenth-century artist to create a haunting work in the *vanitas* genre, showing an owl perched on a human skull. Next to the skull is a candlestick in which the candle's flame is symbolically dying. The term *vanitas* means emptiness, and paintings of this type were meant to emphasize the fleeting nature of vanity and of life itself. They usually included a skull accompanied by reminders of the certainty of death, such as decaying fruit, hour-glasses and insects. In this case the artist, whose name is unknown, made the scene even more sombre and sinister by perching a staring owl, the feared messenger of death, upon the skull.

Sir Walter Scott (1771–1832) continues this theme in his poem 'Ancient Gaelic Melody' (1819), in which he speaks of 'Birds of omen dark and foul, Night-crow, raven, bat, and owl',

'Owl, Skull and Candle', an anonymous Dutch or German *vanitas* painting of the 17th century, oil on panel.

begging them to 'Leave the sick man to his dream – All night long he heard you scream.'[2]

In many images of the owl at this time there is a clear link between the owl and witchcraft. It is more common for that rival nocturnal killer, the cat, to act as the witch's familiar, but

occasionally the cat is displaced by the owl, sometimes depicted riding calmly on the handle of the witch's broom as she flies through the night sky.

As we move into modern times the evil owl begins to lose its power, but it still lurks in a few dark corners. What often happens when an ancient symbol of wickedness begins to go into decline is that it moves from serious belief to comic relief. Halloween is a good example of this. Originally a pagan celebration of the Celtic New Year, when the boundary between the living and the dead became blurred, the dead became dangerous for a brief while and the living defended themselves by mimicking the evil spirits to placate them. Today children use this as an excuse to dress up as ghouls or witches to frighten adults. The solemn ceremonies of yesterday have become little more than light-hearted pantomime. Among the imagery involved in these Halloween displays are all the ghosts, goblins, zombies, demons and other monsters of the modern horror genre. One of the wicked animals that accompany these evil spirits, acting as a witch's familiar, is the owl.

It is possible today to buy a witch's hat so voluminous that it has enough room for an owl to set up a nest inside it. The owl's face peers out of the hat and, in so doing, manages to keep alive the old tradition of the evil owl of ancient times. It may now be no more than a joke, but it is a joke with a long history behind it and shows that, although the wicked owl is no longer taken seriously as a harbinger of death and destruction, it has not been completely forgotten.

THE OBSTINATE OWL

In the seventeenth century a new kind of owl symbol became popular, that of the obstinate owl. It appears in 1602 and again

At full moon, a Spanish witch returns home, her owl familiar perched on the broomstick.

The owl as a symbol of blindness in the light: an etching from George Wither's *A Collection of Emblemes, Ancient and Moderne* (1635).

in 1635 as an etching depicting the owl as the owner of eyesight that declines in efficiency as the intensity of the light increases. It shows the owl wearing spectacles and carrying flaming torches, one in each claw. In front of it stands a pair of candlesticks with brightly burning candles. In the sky, the sun shines down on the scene and the moral is that, if someone has a blind prejudice, no amount of enlightened reasoning will enable him to see the folly of his ways. In fact, the more reasoned argument is presented to him the more stubborn his prejudice will become. The epigram reads *He that is blind will nothing see, What light so e're about him be.* The poem below the emblem begins:

It is by some supposed that our Owls,
By Day-time are no perfect sighted Fowls;
And that the more you do augment the light,
The more you shall deprive them of their sight.
Nor candles, Torches, nor the sun at noon,
Nor spectacles, nor all of these in one,
Can make an Owlet in the day-time see,
Though none, by night, hath better eyes than she.[3]

Owl in Parliament:
Oliver Cromwell
dissolves the
English 'Rump'
Parliament on
19 April 1653,
here shown in a
Dutch print. After
this dissolution
Cromwell became
Lord Protector with
dictatorial powers.

A little later in the seventeenth century the obstinate owl reappears in a famous Dutch print showing Oliver Cromwell dismissing the English Parliament in 1653. Angered by their refusal to see the need for reforms, he entered the Chamber and hurled abuse at them calling them drunkards, whoremasters and corrupt and unjust men. Aided by forty musketeers, he had the members of Parliament driven from the chamber, some by force. In the Dutch print we see them being herded out and at their head is an owl wearing spectacles and a large iron collar on which there is a lighted candle. The use of the owl in this dramatic scene was meant to underline the fact that the members of Parliament who were leaving the chamber had been blind to the need to make essential reforms, despite repeated requests that they should do so. Again the owl was being employed as a symbol of obstinacy and wilful blindness.

THE OWL AS A VEHICLE

In Asia in the Hindu religion the owl has a complex dualistic symbolism. Its primary role is as a *vahana*, a divine vehicle or mount, on which a goddess can ride. The deity in question is Lakshmi, the goddess of wealth and prosperity, and her owl is called Uluka or Ulooka in Sanskrit. In spite of the owl's association with the goddess it is still looked upon in an unfavourable light by Indians in general, who see it as a bird of ill omen and a messenger of bad luck. They believe that if an owl visits a house something evil will happen there.

Owls are viewed as having an unusual lifestyle, involving loneliness, fear and isolation. In this respect they are said to be like the very rich, who shut themselves off from ordinary day-to-day living. So the presence of an owl as the carrier for the goddess Lakshmi is a constant reminder to her that although she represents great wealth she must at the same time guard against its pitfalls. She must represent generous wealth, or spiritual wealth, and avoid the selfishness of the lonely miser. When the goddess descends to earth to visit the poor, on one special night

The goddess Lakshmi with her owl, in an Indian popular print.

Long-legged owl, a mid-20th-century brass figure made by a local artist in Mumbai, India.

in the year, to take away the darkness of poverty, she rides on her great white owl because her steed, being a bird of the night, will know the darkest places to which it can carry her, and where she can therefore do the most good.

Confusingly, in the northern Indian city of Ludhiana, owls are caught and killed every year to honour the goddess Lakshmi during the festival of Divali. A local headline reads: 'Divali spells doom for owls in Ludhiana. Hapless birds sacrificed to appease Goddess Lakshmi.' Owl-catchers are able to sell the birds to individuals who are suffering from financial problems, and who believe that the sacrifice of the owls will please the goddess of prosperity, who will then solve their problems for them. A report claims that the owl-catchers are approached every year by 'disillusioned industrialists' with requests that they perform black magic involving the body parts of owls: the flesh, beak, claws, feathers and blood. Why the destruction of the very bird on which Lakshmi relies for her movements through the skies will please the goddess is not at all clear. Logically, the ritual slaughter of owls, robbing her of her sacred vehicle, should make her sad or angry, so this is yet another complication in the contradictory role of the owl in the Hindu religion.

For many Indians owls are also symbols of laziness, because they appear to sit around doing nothing. A wife whose husband is not pulling his weight with household chores may be described by her as 'sitting round like an owl'. Despite this the small brass images of owls that are sold in India today look remarkably sprightly and ready to spring into action.

Taken together, these attitudes towards the owl in India add up to something closer to the ancient view of the wicked bird rather than the wise one. And yet, at the same time, Uluka is accepted as a trusty beast of burden for the beloved goddess of prosperity and even, occasionally, for her companion Shiva. Curious ambiguities of this kind are not unknown in other aspects of the Hindu religion, which may be one of the reasons why Westerners find its tenets rather hard to grasp.

THE WISE OWL

Today the most popular view of the owl is that he is a friendly, wise old bird. As we have seen, the owl as a sorcerer and a messenger of doom has largely been relegated to a superstitious past. Thanks to natural history books and television programmes we are all much too familiar with the wonders of bird life today to be able, even in fantasy, to see the owl as anything other than an avian marvel. In moments when we set aside our scientific objectivity and allow ourselves to indulge in a little romantic make-believe, we find ourselves compelled to see the owl in a more kindly light.

The reason we select wisdom as the special quality of this particular bird is due simply to the human shape of its head. Its broad face with a pair of huge, solemn eyes blinking at us gives the impression that, like us, its brain is packed with higher centres that give it a level of intelligence far beyond that of other avian species. A bird it may be, but bird-brained it is not. As a result, in countless myths, legends and tall tales, the owl is featured as the epitome of clever thinking. A classic example is the story of the mice and the owl by La Fontaine.[4] This tells us about an ingenious owl that lived in a hollow pine. Inside the tree

> Were found full many footless mice,
> But well provision'd, fat, and nice.
> The bird had bit off all their feet,
> And fed them there with heaps of wheat.
> That this owl reason'd, who can doubt?
> When to the chase he first went out,
> And home alive the vermin brought,
> Which in his talons he had caught,
> The nimble creatures ran away.
> Next time, resolved to make them stay,
> He cropp'd their legs, and found, with pleasure,
> That he could eat them at his leisure;
> It were impossible to eat
> Them all at once, did health permit.
> His foresight, equal to our own,
> In furnishing their food was shown.

The mice and the owl: an engraving by J. J. Grandville for the 1841 edition of Jean de La Fontaine's *Fables Choisies* (verses first published in 1678).

The suggestion here is that the owl was using a reasoning power similar to our own and that it was capable of developing a kind of animal husbandry in which it kept legless mice alive and fattened them up so that it could make a meal of them when its nocturnal hunting was failing to provide new kills. La Fontaine added a note to this poem insisting that it was based on observational fact. As this is clearly nonsensical it is worth asking how such a claim could have come about. In such cases there are usually separate fragments of fact that, when combined, are allowed to add up to much more than the sum of their parts. It has been claimed that some owls may store a few freshly killed surplus rodents for later consumption. It has also been noted that some mice will feign death, going limp when they are caught by the owl, only to make a dash for freedom when the bird relaxes its grip. And third, owls are said to have been observed biting through the feet of mice that have been trapped by their legs, to free them before devouring them. If these three isolated facts – storing mice in a larder, finding them sometimes alive after they have been caught, and biting through their imprisoned limbs to release them from metal traps – are combined, it is only a short step to create a scenario in which the owl has become a clever livestock farmer. As so often happens, there are grains of truth in even the most outlandish tales of animal activities and it is these grains that explain how a myth can have been born and then allowed to grow and develop a life of its own.

This romantic vision of the owl as a bird of great sagacity is over 2,000 years old. As we have seen it began as a major force in ancient Greece, but it is not clear whether it flourished in modern times because of a respect for ancient Greece and a growing scholarly knowledge of Grecian society, or whether it developed independently out of the major shift of attitude towards animals that occurred during the Victorian period. It was then, during the nineteenth century, that animal welfare first became a major issue and special societies were set up to prevent animal abuses and to promote a more caring attitude towards other species.

Whichever is the case, it is certainly true that the Victorians generally viewed the owl as a wise rather than an evil bird. In *Punch* magazine in 1875 appeared the following rhyme:

There was an owl lived in an oak,
The more he heard the less he spoke,
The less he spoke the more he heard –
O, if men were all like that wise bird.[5]

In modern times the wise, friendly owl still makes a symbolic appearance on certain special occasions. At Scottish weddings a live owl is sometimes required to be present at the ceremony. Its role is to deliver the wedding rings to the best man. At the start of the service, the owl sits on its perch at the back of the church,

A wedding owl at a ceremony at Balgonie Castle, Fife, Scotland, 8 October 2008.

alongside its trainer. When the best man is asked for the rings, he turns and the owl is released and silently flies the length of the church to settle on his arm. On one of the bird's legs there is a leather strap carrying the two rings for the bride and groom. These are untied and handed to the officiating priest. In this way, when the young couple put on the rings they feel that they are being blessed with the wisdom of the owl.

For the record, the sad truth is that, scientifically speaking, the owl is not the most intelligent of birds. Its wisdom is simply an illusion created by its physical appearance. Intelligence in animals is related to their way of life, with opportunists always being more intelligent than specialists. The opportunists – birds like the crows – have no special survival device and must rely on their wits every day, trying out every trick in the book to survive. To give just one example, a crow learned to drop hard nuts, that it could not open with its beak, on to a main road where they were run over and broken by passing cars. It even learned to drop them on a pedestrian crossing, so that it could collect the broken nuts when the traffic stopped and it could avoid being run over itself. It is inconceivable that an owl could display this level of intelligence. As with all birds of prey, it has evolved the highly specialized sense organs and refined physical attributes that make it such an efficient killer that it does not face the daily survival challenges of the opportunist. Like a snake, it can strike, feed and rest.

THE PROTECTIVE OWL

The owl has yet another symbolic role. In this it matters little whether its personality is evil or saintly. This is because the owl is now acting as a security guard and providing this protective owl is on your side you care little whether it is a demon or a scholar, just so long as it defends you against attack.

Several different animals have been used in the past as amulets or charms to protect their owner from ill fortune or evil spirits. Despite its association with death and disaster the owl has been employed in this way and it is easy to see why. If an owl is the herald of death, then if you wear a lucky owl you can imagine its powers being directed towards your enemy instead of towards yourself. In other words if the owl is a frightening creature you can use it to frighten your opponents.

A protective owl key-ring, made from the carved and painted wood of the Spindle Tree. Ainu culture, Japan, 20th century.

Some Asiatic peoples, such as the Turks and the Mongols, are known to keep an owl near the cradle of a sick child in the belief that it will frighten away the evil spirits that are causing the illness.

The Ainu people in Japan make wooden images of eagle owls and nail them to their houses to protect the occupants in times of famine or epidemic. Even today the owl is employed as a lucky charm by the Ainu and it is possible to buy a hand-carved wooden owl figure to carry on a talismanic key-ring and chain. Made from the red wood of the Japanese spindle tree and decorated with gold and green colouring, this highly stylized owl image is believed to keep watch not just over the owner but also his entire village. A larger model, created by the whole community, is sometimes erected as 'the defender of the village'.

Strangely the Ainu do not view all kinds of owls as protective. Some are seen as downright evil. These are believed to be harmful to man and able to tell a good man from a bad one. If one is caught it will look at a good man with open eyes, but will only peer at a bad one through nearly closed eyes. Staring with open eyes is called 'searching out the man' (*ainu oro wande*); peering through slit eyes is called 'man-ignoring' (*ainu eshpa*). And heaven help the man who sees the shape of a flying owl crossing the face of the moon, for this means that the impending evil is going to be serious, so much so that the man

concerned may have to change his name to hide from the approaching demon.

On the other side of the world, on the Balearic island of Minorca in the Mediterranean, the owl is also used as a protective device. Even today it is the most popular amulet or lucky charm among the Minorcans, who may wear it around the neck in the form of a pendant or place it as a ceramic figure in their houses to ward off demonic spirits or to outstare the malevolent Evil Eye. It is sometimes reduced to little more than a pair of bulging, round eyes and a small beak, with the body largely omitted. This simplification emphasizes that it is the large eyes that are thought to be the important element in the task of outstaring the Evil Eye. The larger Minorcan protective owls, placed in the houses to protect the occupants from misfortune, are usually made from white ceramic covered in brightly coloured detail in red, orange, purple, green and blue.

There is no denying that symbolically the owl is truly versatile. As a nocturnal predator it is evil; with its (supposedly) poor daylight vision it is blindly obstinate; with its swift, elegant flight it is a vehicle for the gods; with its solemn expression it is wise, and with its powerful weapons it is an efficient protector. Few other animals can boast so many contrasting symbolic roles. No wonder the owl has had such a long and complex involvement in human mythology.

5 Emblematic Owls

Today many organizations employ the owl as an emblem, placing its image on a badge, a flag, a sign or a crest to provide themselves with an attractive visual logo that identifies them and sets them apart from their rivals. A sports club may display it as a predatory bird, emphasizing the sharp talons as it swoops down for the kill. A learned society may depict it in its guise as the wise old owl, employing it as a symbol of knowledge. This modern use of the owl as an emblematic figure has a long history, stretching back to the sixteenth century and beyond.

The cult of illustrated emblem books began in 1531 with the publication of the *Emblematum Liber* of Andrea Alciati.[1] His idea was to make moral points in the form of illustrated poems, borrowing heavily on ancient fables and moral tales but his special contribution was to condense these tales into epigrams and pictures. He felt that if he could express the moral concept briefly and elegantly it would be possible for artists to 'fashion the kind of thing we call badges and which we fasten on hats, or use as trademarks'. In a revised edition of his book that appeared in 1534 the pictures were reorganized so that emblems were presented one per page. This idea became so popular that many more books of emblems appeared in the centuries that followed and a whole genre of pictorial moralizing was developed.

ANDREÆ ALCIATI

Senex puellam amans.

EMBLEMA CXVI.

The owl and corpse, the young girl and old man, in a woodcut illustration from Andrea Alciati's *Emblemata* (1584): 'Like the horned owl standing upon cadavers, so sits our girl next to Sophocles.'

Dvm *Sophocles (quamuis affecta ætate) puellam*
A quæstu Archippen ad sua vota trahit,
Allicit & pretio, tulit ægrè insana iuuentus
Ob zelum, & tali carmine vtrumque notat:
Noctua vt in tumulis, super vtque cadauera bubo,
Talis apud Sophoclem nostra puella sedet.

Id ex Athenæo lib. 13. Dipnosoph. Ex quo disci-
mus turpissimum esse seni amore diffluere: quod
& Deo & ipsi etiam naturæ odiosum esse nostri di-
ctitant. Notum illud Ouidij,
Turpe senex miles, turpe senilis amor.

To give one example of Alciati's original emblems, no. 116 shows an elderly man fondling the naked left breast of a young girl. They are seated beneath a tree and on the ground next to them is an owl standing on the chest of a corpse. This strange scene symbolizes the idea that it is wrong for a young girl to give herself to a man who is so old that he is almost a corpse. The Latin poem accompanying the illustration reveals that the author is making the point that an elderly man (in this case the aged Sophocles) should not use his power and his riches to seduce a young woman: 'Like the night-owl perched on the tombs, and like the horned-owl standing upon the cadaver, so sits our girl next to Sophocles.' Here the owl is being used symbolically in a rather unusual way. Because it is a living thing that is associated with graveyards (where it may be observed flitting about at night) it is thought of as being somehow related to the dead. So, emblematically, with a leap of the imagination, it becomes the full-of-life young girl who is associating with the one-foot-in-the-grave old

The owl breaks the silence of the night with its cries, a woodcut illustration for Guillaume de La Perrière's *Morosophie* (1553).

'SIC VIVO' –
Thus I live: one of
Pierre Woeiriot's
engraved illustra-
tions for Georgette
de Montenay's
*Emblematum
Christianorum
centuria* (1584).

xxj.

Pingue olenm ſitiens, exoſam lampada bubo
Non tamen ipſe ſua comprimit ante manu.
Et Satan, Veri impatiens, inimica malorum
Sæuus in inſontes commouet arma ducum.

man. This symbolism of the owl as a young girl did not catch on,
however, and does not appear anywhere else in myth or folklore
as far as I can ascertain.

A slightly later version of this literary genre was Guillaume
de La Perrière's *Morosophie* (1553).[2] It was the first bilingual book
of emblems, having the text in both Latin and French. In one of
the illustrations a couple are shown in a state of shock, having
been awoken by the weird hooting of an owl that perches in a tree
right outside their open door. In translation, the text reads: 'As

the bird that babbles under the deep night desires to disturb those whom sleep refreshes, so the evil tongue desiring to pour out evil poison does so, so that sound minds should moan having lost their calm.' Clearly, here the owl is being depicted as a sinister creature of the night, disturbing the slumber of honest folk with its eerie, haunting cries.

One of the followers of this publishing phenomenon was Georgette de Montenay, described by some as a proto-feminist, who in 1584 produced a volume of 100 Christian emblems.[3] It was the first book of emblems to employ incised engravings instead of the more usual woodcuts for the illustrations. These engravings, by Pierre Woeiriot, made it possible to create more precise and detailed images. Among them is a curious example of owl symbolism, in which the bird is depicted holding a severed hand on the end of a long stick. With this hand it reaches out towards a burning lamp, trying to touch the hot oil in the lamp with the dead fingers. The title of the picture is *SIC VIVO – Thus I live*. The explanation offered for this odd scene is that 'Longing for some of the oil in the burning lamp, the owl does not risk using its own claws'. This is meant to symbolize the way in which Satan, unable to face a difficult problem directly, instead moves the brutal arms of evil leaders against the innocent. Since the owl in this scenario must stand for the Devil, this example of the emblematic owl must be harking back to the evil owl of folklore.

In 1635 an Oxford scholar called George Wither produced *A Collection of Emblemes, Ancient and Moderne*, with the texts in English. Wither had gone up to Magdalen College, Oxford, at the age of sixteen and would go on to become a prolific and outspoken author who was imprisoned more than once for the way he expressed his views. His book of emblems is full of sound advice in the form of what were called 'silent parables',

the allegorical pictures to which he attached his epigrams and poems. Several of these depicted owls and each one showed the bird in a different emblematic role. One example shows an owl with outspread wings standing on top of a *caduceus*, a snake-entwined staff that later became the symbol of medicine.[4] Mercury and Pallas stand on either side, each holding a cornucopia. In this context the owl symbolizes the night and the epigram that accompanies the picture is: 'Before thou bring thy Works to Light, Consider on them, in the Night.' In other words think hard about what you are saying before you rush into print. In the poem beneath the picture, the author points out that the cornucopia signify a wealth created by 'studious watchfulness which, here, the Bird of Athens signifies'. And he concludes with

the words 'By Night, we best may ruminate upon Our Purposes .
. . For, of the World-without, when most we see, Then, blindest
to the World-within, are we.'

This idea of the owl as a creature of the dark night who is not
troubled by frantic daytime chaos and who therefore has time
to ponder and contemplate is an interesting one because it may
go part of the way towards explaining the owl as a symbol of
wisdom. It may not be simply the human-shaped head of the
bird that makes it seem wise, but also the fact that it is awake
at a time when it can avoid the alarms and confusions of the
day. Another emblematic owl in Wither's collection symbolizes
the British love of the stiff upper lip.[5] Here the owl represents
stoicism and calm in the face of fury. The picture shows an owl

The owl as a
symbol of calm, in
Wither's *Collection
of Emblemes*.

sitting quietly on a perch while being mobbed by angry birds
and the epigram instructs that 'We best shall quiet clamorous
Throngs, When we ourselves can rule our Tongues.' The author
expands on this theme in the accompanying poem:

When I observe the Melancholic Owls,
Considering with what patience they sustain
The many clamours of the greater Fowls;
And how the little Chirpers they disdain . . .
Me thinks by their example I am taught
To sleight the slanders of Injurious Tongues;
To set the scoffs of censurers at naught,
And with a brave neglect to bear our wrongs.

The owl as
a symbol of
wisdom, in
Wither's *Collection
of Emblemes.*

His third owl emblem portrays the owl as a symbol of wisdom and learning. It shows an owl standing on an open book, with the epigram 'By Study and by Watchfulness, The Gem of Knowledge we possess'.[6] The poem beneath the emblem is a prolonged plea to students to avoid lust, unlawful appetites and sottishness. If they fail to do this he concludes, 'You are not what the Athenian owl implies, But what our English owlet signifies.' It is not surprising to see the owl of Athens put forward by Wither as the symbol of wisdom, but why the poor little English owlet should be made to represent a lustful, lawless drunkard is not at all clear.

Wither's fourth owl emblem is a more sombre image, with the owl here standing on a human skull.[7] The epigram above it

The owl as a symbol of mortality, in Wither's *Collection of Emblemes.*

68

states 'Whilst thou dost here enjoy thy breath, Continue mindful of thy Death.' The poem enlarges on this theme, warning the reader not to put off until tomorrow the things that should be done today, because our time on Earth is so limited. The role of the owl here is that of the melancholy night-bird that inhabits graveyards and is associated with death.

Leaping forward in time we come to a very different kind of owl emblem, a badge worn by the leader of a girls' scouting group. The Girl Guides movement, the female equivalent of the Boy Scouts, was founded in 1910 and it soon became clear that younger girls (seven to ten years) also wanted to join and that they needed a separate organization to suit their age. It was decided to call them Brownies, after the helpful children in a story by Juliana Horatia Ewing, written in 1870. The Brownie movement started officially in 1914 and the adult leader of a Brownie Pack was called a Brown Owl. She wore a special badge, a Girl Guide Brown Owl Pin Warrant Badge, showing the head of a brown owl with long curving ear tufts. Early examples of these owl pins have now become collectors' items. A Brown Owl Blanket Patch spelled out in some detail what qualities were expected from a Brown Owl. Stared at by a small owl with a somewhat startled expression, the words on the blanket patch read: Brave, Reliable, Organized, Wonderful, Nice, Outward, Wise and Loveable. As a symbolically virtuous owl this would take some beating. Brown Owl was sometimes assisted by individuals known as Tawny Owl or Snowy Owl. When asked why their leaders were called owls, one of the Brownies replied: 'Because of the Brownie story. Tommy and Betty went to the wise owl in the wood and she guided them to do the right thing.'

In more modern times the owl is still widely used as an emblem, but today the thinking behind its selection as an appropriate symbol is less precise. For example, in Barcelona a company that installs neon lighting erected a huge owl on top of a building on the Avinguda Diagonal at the point where it meets Passeig de Sant Joan. The idea was simply to use the intense stare of the owl's eyes as a way of advertising bright neon lighting. When it was first put up it emitted hypnotizing circles of light from its eyes all through the night. In 2003 this lighting effect was stopped – possibly because it was too intimidating for nocturnal Catalans – but the bird itself remains in place, one of the largest owl images in the world.

In the realm of politics the emblematic owl was introduced as a minor theme in the McCain/Obama election struggle in 2008. Outsider artist Andrew Mass created an old McCain owl to compete with a sporty Obama bluebird. With both birds perched on a branch labelled Honesty and Truth, he invites you

Obama vs. McCain by Andrew Mass, an Outsider artist, Illinois, 2008. This coloured ink sketch juxtaposes the old owl McCain and the bluebird Obama, both perched on the limb of honesty and truth.

to choose between the aged wisdom of McCain the owl and the streamlined youthful vigour of Obama the bluebird.

At least three regions of the world have employed the owl as their official emblem. In Canada the province of Manitoba adopted the great grey owl (*Strix nebulosa*) as its official bird emblem on 16 July 1987. A year-round resident of Manitoba, the great grey can be found throughout the mixed wood and coniferous forests of the province. Further to the west, the province of Alberta also has an owl as official emblem, but it is the great horned owl (*Bubo virginianus*). Its original coat of arms was a shield, the design of which was given to them in 1907 by King Edward VII, but in 1977 the province's schoolchildren chose an additional emblem. They voted for the owl as the official bird and the legislature approved their choice on the grounds that, 'a resourceful and resilient bird, the great horned owl exemplifies the best traits of Alberta's people, both past and present.' Today a Disneyfied version of the owl, called Wugie the Owl, has become a sports mascot in Edmonton, the capital of the province. Wugie stands for World University Games in Edmonton. In the east of Canada the National Assembly of the province of Quebec also chose an owl as their official bird. In their case it is the snowy owl (*Nyctea scandiaca*), an appropriate species to represent the icy wastes in the north of their region. As with Manitoba, their choice was made in 1987 when there was a major national movement to enhance the quality of the environment and save wild species.

Several sports teams have adopted the owl as their mascot. In the United States Philadelphia's Temple University teams are called the Temple Owls. This name comes from Temple's early days, when it was a night school. It is clear from the logo that the feature of the bird that they are emphasizing is not its wisdom but its lightning strike. The owl is shown in the act of swooping down with an angry frown on its face, its sharp beak open and its massive claws ready to grasp its prey. Unfortunately the artist who designed the logo did not know his owls very well as he has given their bird the feet of an eagle, with three toes pointing forward and one pointing back, instead of the typical owl arrangement of two forward and two back (zygodactylous).

Wugie the Owl, the sports mascot of Edmonton, Alberta, for the 1983 World University Games organized by FISU.

Also in America the world of professional ice hockey has employed the owl emblem. The Columbus Owls played at the Fairgrounds Coliseum in the Ohio State Fairgrounds at Columbus, Ohio until 1977, when they relocated to Dayton Ohio and became the Dayton Owls, keeping the same owl emblem. They then moved on to become the Grand Rapids Owls until 1980 when they finally collapsed as a team. Even then their owl emblem managed to survive; it was taken over by the Grand Rapids Junior Owls Hockey Club when the owners of the Junior Owls asked for and received permission to use the Owls' name and logo. This is a case of an emblem becoming more successful than the clubs it represented.

Temple Owls, sports emblem of Temple University, Philadelphia.

In England the sports team with the owl as its official emblem is Sheffield Wednesday Football Club, established in 1867. The team became professional twenty years later, and its original nickname was the Blades, because Sheffield was a famous centre for the manufacture of knives. Then, at the start of the twentieth century, one of their players presented them with an owl mascot to honour their stadium at Owlerton and, from that point on, they became known as the Owls. (The original nickname of the Blades was taken over by their rivals, Sheffield United.) The first club badge with their new emblem showed a rather shy little owl sitting in a tree, but in modern times this has been replaced by a much more powerful looking bird, based apparently on the Egyptian owl hieroglyph, showing the body of the bird in profile with the head turned full face.

Another northern English football club briefly adopted the owl as its emblem. In 1964 Leeds United borrowed the owl from the city crest, which showed three owls, two wearing coronets. The city crest itself was based on the family crest of Sir John Saville, first alderman of Leeds. Although the football club owl emblem did not last long (perhaps overshadowed by the

Owls football emblem of Sheffield Wednesday Football Club.

Sheffield owl) the city owl remains the proud emblem of Leeds to this day and outside the civic offices in the city centre is a magnificent golden owl statue. A third northern English football club also has an owl emblem. Like Leeds, Oldham Athletic took its owl from the local crest, but does not use 'Owls' as their nickname, in deference to the supporters of Sheffield Wednesday. The Oldham owl is a 'canting' reference, or heraldic pun, on the old pronunciation of the town's name – Owldham.

Heraldic Owls: Leeds City Council Crest.

Slovenia, a country that won its independence only as recently as 1991, needed a new mascot to help in its bid for the 26th Winter Universiade that will take place in 2013. It chose the owl, or rather the highly stylized eyes and beak of an owl. The owl was selected for several reasons: because it represents knowledge and intelligence, because its flight is silent and elegant, because it is common in the Slovenian forests and even in the Slovenian towns, and, rather charmingly, because it is a nocturnal bird, suggesting that the Universiade is a sporting event that does not end at sunset but carries on into nights of socializing.

Nagano Snowlets: Japanese Olympic emblem.

There are other sporty owls right across the globe. In Podolsk on the outskirts of Moscow is an owl dressed as a defending ice hockey player, its 'owlness' all but obliterated. And there is even a sporting owl emblem in Japan. The Japanese Nagano Snowlets, a group of four baby owls, has been described by one critic as the worst mascot in Olympic history. One of the owlets is blue and purple, another green and orange, a third blue and green and the fourth purple and orange. All four have bright yellow eyes and, were it not for their spindly legs, would look better in the sumo ring than on the sports field.

So iconic is the basic shape of the owl that it can be exploited emblematically in many different ways. A thorough search, country by country, would probably unearth literally hundreds of owl emblems, not only at sports clubs but also at night clubs

opposite: Golden Owl: Leeds City owl statue.

and supermarkets, shops and businesses. The thought-provoking, complex owl emblems of earlier centuries have been superseded by the simple-minded, crude images of modern commerce. As fascinating wild birds that deserve our respect and protection, owls may have seen their status raised today, but as emblems it has to be said that something has been lost.

6 Literary Owls

Owls have landed on many a page, from the earliest fables to the comic writings of Edward Lear, A. A. Milne and James Thurber. In one of its first appearances the literary owl features twice in Aesop's fables, written in the sixth century BC. Aesop was a story-telling slave in ancient Greece who used animal tales to make moral statements. The first owl story, 'The Owl and the Birds', concerns the way in which the ordinary birds ignore the wise warnings of the owl. Later, when they are proved wrong and the owl is proved to have been right, they turn to it for pearls of wisdom, but the owl is now silent and 'no longer gives them advice, but in solitude laments their past folly'.

In the second owl fable, 'The Owl and the Grasshopper', an owl who is trying to sleep during the day is disturbed by the grasshopper's incessant chirping. Simple requests for peace and quiet are refused by the grasshopper, so the owl is driven to employing a trick, saying to the grasshopper: 'Since I cannot sleep, on account of your song which, believe me, is as sweet as the lyre of Apollo, I shall indulge myself in drinking some nectar which Pallas lately gave me. If you do not dislike it, come to me and we will drink it together.' The grasshopper found this offer hard to refuse, flew up and was promptly killed and eaten by the owl, who could now enjoy some silent slumber. The moral of this story is that flattery does not mean that you are admired.

To these two original owl fables many more were added over the centuries. One of the earliest comes from the *Panchatantra*, an Indian collection of animal fables in verse and prose sometimes called the *Fables of Bidpai*. The original text has long been lost but is believed to have been written as early as the third century AD. In the tale of the owl's coronation all the birds gathered in the forest to complain about the fact that their king, the great bird-god Garuda, was no longer carrying out his duties towards them. He had become so obsessed with serving Visnu that the birds felt neglected and wished to elect a new king who would look after them properly. The owl, looking so wise and solemn, seemed the obvious choice, so the birds set about preparing for his coronation. They decorated his throne with leaves, flowers and animal skins, arranged for maidens to sing songs of praise and for festive music to play as the owl was led in procession to the place of his anointment.

As the honoured bird sat down on his throne, awaiting the ceremony, there was an interruption. A raucous crow, making a great noise, landed near the throne and demanded to know what was going on. The other birds, still uncertain about their choice of the owl as the new king, sought the crow's advice. He was, after all, a very intelligent bird, and his opinion could not be ignored. When they told the crow about the imminent coronation of the owl, the great black bird laughed in disbelief. He dismissed the idea, saying that the owl was blind during the day, when he would be unable to rule. He also pointed out that since the owl could see at night when the other birds could not, they would be completely at his mercy during the hours of darkness. What was more, Garuda would hardly be pleased by this development. It was a thoroughly bad idea to have two kings at the same time and since Garuda had already made a name for himself and had great influence it would be much better to leave him to rule alone.

Listening to this, the birds lost their nerve and decided that perhaps, after all, they had made a bad mistake. So they silently dispersed, unnoticed by the owl, whose eyes were blinded by the strong daylight. After a long delay the owl sensed that something was amiss and demanded to know why the ceremony had stopped. He was told that everyone had gone because the crow had disrupted the proceedings. Only the crow remained and the owl turned on him and told him in no uncertain terms that, from now on, owls and crows would be sworn enemies and that this hatred would last forever. After this outburst, the owl went angrily away and the crow was left to ponder on what he had done. He had told the truth as he saw it but the result was that he had created an unwanted and unnecessary enemy for life. The owl was harmless and the crow had thoughtlessly stirred up anger for no good reason. He felt he had acted foolishly and regretted his impulsive behaviour. He may have been right but it had cost him dear to say so.

In this old tale, the symbolism of the owl and the crow is intriguing. The wise owl is vain, with limited powers, and the crow is sharp and clever but impulsive and lacking in any sort of diplomacy. Both end up losers. The moral seems to be that a man with limited abilities should accept his shortcomings and that a man with a clever brain must learn some social skills.

In the seventeenth century the French poet La Fontaine gathered together many of these early fables and adapted them to his own style, adding some new fables of his own. In 'The Owl and the Eagle' he tells of a pact of friendship between these two great birds. Sworn enemies in the past, they now agree never to attack one another's chicks. The only problem is: how will they identify them? The owl tells the eagle that in his case that is easy because his chicks are so beautiful, 'Well formed and fine, with pretty sparkling eyes'. One day, later on, the eagle comes across the nest of the owl's chicks and, taking a close look at them decides that they are 'grim little monsters, fitted but to shock' and therefore cannot be the chicks of his friend and promptly devours the lot. When the owl discovers what has happened he is outraged and demands the punishment of the eagle for breaking their pact. But it is pointed out to him that it is he who is to blame for exaggerating the beauty of his nestlings. The moral of this tale is that children always look beautiful to their parents but not necessarily to anyone else.

In the eighteenth century the English author John Gay took up the baton of fable-telling and in 1727 published *Fifty-one Fables in Verse*. In one of these two grumpy old owls are bewailing the fact that they are no longer treated with proper respect, as their forebears were, back in the days of ancient Athens:

Athens, the seat of learned fame,
With general voice revered our name;
On merit title was conferred,
And all adored the Athenian bird.
. . . But now, alas! we're quite neglected,
And a pert sparrow's more respected.

A sparrow, overhearing this nostalgic moaning, roundly attacks the old owls with the criticism that birds have now learned that looks can be misleading and that just because the owls happen to appear wise and venerable does not necessarily mean that they are so. He goes on to say that if they concentrate on what they are good at, namely catching mice, the farmers will applaud them and they will gain true respect for the labours rather than false respect for their looks.

Another fable popular in the eighteenth century concerned a vain young owl who felt that he was so handsome that only the daughter of an eagle would do for his bride. When he heard of this, the eagle treated the suggestion with scorn but said that he would give his consent if the owl would meet him the following day, at sunrise, high in the sky. The conceited young owl agreed to do this but when the time came found himself so dazzled by the bright rays of the morning sun that he became dizzy and fell to the ground, landing on some rocks where he was promptly mobbed by angry daytime birds. The moral of this fable is that ambition without talent ends in disgrace.

A nineteenth-century Russian fable tells of a blind donkey that has become caught up in a thicket and cannot escape. It is night-time and a helpful owl guides the donkey to safety. The donkey is so grateful that it begs the owl to accompany it every-where. The owl agrees and enjoys the luxury of sitting on the donkey's back, but then daylight comes and the owl cannot see clearly where they are going. It misdirects the donkey and together they fall into a ravine. Again this tale focuses on the owl's limited skills and the moral is that because someone is brilliant at one thing it does not mean that they will be good at another.

This theme of the owl being wonderful only at night is taken up again in a poem entitled simply 'The Owl' by the English Victorian poet Bryan Waller Procter (1787–1874), who wrote under the name of Barry Cornwall. A shortened version reads:

In the hollow tree, in the grey old tower,
The spectral owl doth dwell;
Dull, hated, despised in the sunshine hour,
But at dusk – he's abroad and well.

Not a bird of the forest e'er mates with him;
All mock him outright by day,

But at night, when the woods grow still and dim,
The boldest will shrink away.
Oh, when the night falls, and roosts the fowl,
Then, then is the reign of the horn-ed owl!

Oh, when the moon shines and the dogs do howl,
Then, then is the cry of the horn-ed owl!
Mourn not for the owl nor his gloomy plight!
The owl hath his share of good;
If a prisoner he be in the broad daylight,
He is lord in the dark green wood.

So when the night falls and dogs do howl,
Sing ho for the reign of the horned owl!
We know not alway who are kings by day,
But the king of the night is the bold brown owl.

Apart from Pablo Picasso, few famous people appear to have kept an owl as a pet. This is not surprising as they are highly unsuitable as household companions unless you happen to live in a barn overrun with rodents. Even then, an owl will not usually find it easy to accept the close attentions of human companions. One of the few exceptions to this general rule concerns the famous British nurse Florence Nightingale. She was visiting the Parthenon in Athens in June 1850, where little owls commonly nested, when she saw, to her horror, a baby owl being tormented by a group of Greek children. It had fallen from its nest and was clearly in need of the nursing skills for which Florence was to become so well known. She rescued it, named it Athena after the Greek goddess, and learned how to feed it. The hatchling was so young that it developed an unusually strong bond of attachment with the 'lady with the lamp' and became

Athena, now a mounted specimen at London's Florence Nightingale Museum.

her devoted friend, so much so that it would sit on her finger to be fed and was trained to enter a cage at her request. After a while, Athena became such an intimate companion that it accompanied Florence Nightingale wherever she went, travelling snugly in her pocket. The bird soon became famous as her trademark, and was notorious for attacking visitors with its sharp beak if approached too closely. But in 1855, when Florence was deeply involved with the preparations for her wartime nursing duties in the Crimea, her family decided to leave the little bird in the attic for a while, thinking that it would be able to rid the place of its infestation of mice. Unfortunately the owl had become so tame that it simply sat and waited for its next meal to be served. When nothing arrived it eventually starved to death on the very day that Florence was due to leave for the war.

When she discovered what had happened to her beloved pet Florence was so devastated that she delayed her departure for two days so that she could make arrangements for the owl to be

Florence Nightingale with her pet owl, Athena; a sketch from her sister's book about the bird.

expertly embalmed. Athena's body was sent to a taxidermist in London and was carefully mounted in a lifelike pose. After this, it remained in Florence's house, a constant if now somewhat unresponsive companion, until her own death in 1910. It then passed through several hands, until in 2004 enough money could be raised to purchase it as a permanent exhibit for the Florence Nightingale Museum at St Thomas Hospital in London, where it remains to this day.

The owl with others listens to the mouse, in John Tenniel's woodcut illustration for *Alice's Adventures in Wonderland* (1865).

One of the strangest nineteenth-century literary offerings concerning an owl must surely be Lady Verney's *Life and Death of Athena, an Owlet from the Parthenon*, privately published in

1855 as a special gift for Florence Nightingale, her sister.[1] A copy of the short book was sent to Florence at the front in the Crimea war zone, to cheer her up when she was suffering from a bad fever. According to her sister the only tears that Florence shed during the chaotic week of her delayed departure were as the little body of the dead owl was put into her hands. 'Poor little beastie', she is reputed to have said, 'it was odd how I loved you.'

When Lewis Carroll's *Alice's Adventures in Wonderland* was published in 1865, one might have expected an owl to play a special role in this animal-rich fantasy, but sadly it only makes a silent appearance in one of John Tenniel's classic illustrations.[2] When a self-important mouse is giving a dry lecture to a wet audience, his listeners include a bored owl with its eyes screwed tight shut. At the point where Alice, lacking tact, mentions the bird-hunting skills of her pet cat, all the birds in the group make their excuses and leave, and that is the last we see of the Wonderland owl.

Also in the nineteenth century Edward Lear's nonsense verses gained enormous popularity for their quirky charm. They lived up to their name, being utter nonsense with no morals to offer at their conclusions. His very first nonsense song (1867) was called 'The Owl and the Pussy-cat' and it introduced another kind of owl altogether. Neither evil nor wise, pompous nor vain, Lear's bird has little of the traditional owl about it. The first verse reads:

The Owl and the Pussy-cat went to sea
In a beautiful pea green boat,
They took some honey, and plenty of money,
Wrapped up in a five pound note.
The Owl looked up to the stars above,

And sang to a small guitar,
'O lovely Pussy! O Pussy my love,
What a beautiful Pussy you are,
You are,
You are!
What a beautiful Pussy you are!'

'The Owl and
the Pussycat',
a drawing by
Edward Lear for
his *Nonsense Verse*
(1871).

In the remaining verses the owl and the cat get married, enjoy a feast and finally, as befits two nocturnal predators, dance in the light of the moon. There is no moral and no reference to the owl's special features, either biological or mythological. This is self-proclaimed nonsense verse and was written simply to cheer up a sick child, Janet Symonds, the daughter of Lear's friends. Despite this, Lear's bird remains one of the best known of all fictional owls.

Edward Lear's fondness for owls is apparent from the number of times he includes one in his drawings and sketches. Another well-known example is his 1846 cartoon of his beard. Lear had a very large beard and amused children by suggesting that it was so big that, if they looked closely, they would find birds nesting in it. To accompany the cartoon, he wrote:

It is just as I feared!
Two owls & a hen,
Four larks & a wren,
Have all built their nests in my beard!

In A. A. Milne's much loved children's book *Winnie-the-Pooh*, published in 1926, an owl, who spelled himself WOL, was clearly a descendent of the wise Athenian owl. There was no trace in WOL's personality of the spooky owl of witchcraft and doom. This was a gentle, respected owl, who lived in a hollow tree in 'an old-world residence of great charm, which was grander than anybody else's', with a front door that boasted both a knocker and a bell-pull. He was a friendly sage who was consulted on difficult questions, and who offered thoughtful advice using longer and longer words that were too difficult for a mere bear to understand. But he meant well and, for Milne's young readers,

'Owls in a Beard', a drawing of 1846 by Edward Lear (1812–88).

introduced the idea of an owl as a helpful, learned and slightly grandparental figure.

The American humourist James Thurber was famous for the primitive, childlike drawings with which he illustrated his writings. Their spontaneity gave them a charm that would have been lost had he tried to improve his technique. On one occasion when he did attempt to do this, he was warned by a colleague that 'If ever you got good you'd be mediocre.' His most famous owl drawing avoids this. Called 'The Owl who was God' it was drawn to accompany a typically bizarre Thurber fable. Although it borrows something from the tale of 'The Owl's Coronation' from the third-century *Panchatantra*, Thurber makes the story very much his own. It can be summarized as follows:

One starless night two moles are accosted by an owl. Astonished that he can detect them even in the pitch darkness, they hurry to tell the other animals of his great

Winnie-the-Pooh gets advice from the wise old owl, in a drawing by E. H. Shepard for A. A. Milne's *Winnie-the-Pooh* (1926).

wisdom. A secretary bird decides to test this and asks the owl for another expression for the word 'namely'. 'To wit' says the owl. 'And why does a lover call on his love?' asks the secretary bird. 'To woo' says the owl. Deeply impressed by the owl's extensive knowledge, the secretary bird tells all the other animals. They decide that the owl must be God and they follow him everywhere he goes. They even follow him when, at high noon, he starts walking down the middle of a highway. Because he cannot see in the bright sunlight he does not notice a truck approaching and is killed along with many of his gullible followers.

Thurber's typically whimsical moral was: 'You can fool too many of the people too much of the time.'

In the literature of the twenty-first century the only author to feature owls in an important fictional context is J. K. Rowling. In her brilliant popular revival of the rather tired subject of witch-craft – the Harry Potter series published between 1997 and 2007 – she enlists a variety of owls to act as messengers between her magical world and the ordinary world of 'muggles'. Harry Potter himself has a female snowy owl called Hedwig. In the films based on the books Hedwig is played by seven different male birds: Gizmo, Kasper, Oops, Swoops, Oh-Oh, Elmo and Bandit. They are all males because male snowy owls are smaller than females and therefore easier for a young actor to handle and there are seven of them because, apparently, professional owls have their off-days and stand-ins are frequently needed. Harry's friend Ron has a Eurasian pygmy owl called Pigwidgeon, or Pig for short. There are several other owls in the books, including a huge Eurasian eagle owl, owned by the Malfoy family, and Errol, an elderly male great grey owl, belonging to the Weasley family, who is extremely clumsy and keeps crashing into things when trying to land. We are assured that all violent accidents were the work of a dummy, stunt owl.

It would be easy to argue that it is a shame to see these beautiful owls once again being dragged back into the superstitious, supernatural world of witches and curses that should have vanished centuries ago, but the saving grace of the Harry Potter stories is that they are clearly meant to be read purely as children's fairy stories and not to be taken seriously. So no damage is done. Or, as they say in all Hollywood credits these days, no birds were harmed during the making of these films.

7 Tribal Owls

All over the world there are tribal legends and superstitions about owls, stories that have managed to survive into the twenty-first century. In some cases the tribes involved are still stubbornly clinging on to their traditional way of life but, even where they are adapting to a more modern lifestyle, the old tales of wise owls and witch's owls are still told.

Even in modern Europe, where the ancient tribes have long ago merged into larger nations, one only has to go out into the more remote rural districts to find owl myths and rituals operating at an almost medieval level, with the old beliefs refusing to die away. In Transylvania, for example, farmers in some regions still believe that walking around their fields naked will scare away owls. In Wales if an owl is heard calling among the houses it means that an unmarried girl has lost her virginity. In Russia some hunters carry a lucky charm in the form of owl claws so that, if they are killed, their souls can use the claws to climb up to heaven. In Poland if a married woman dies she will turn into an owl. In France if a pregnant woman hears an owl, she will give birth to a girl. Also in France, in Bordeaux, you must throw salt on the fire to avoid the owl's curse. On the other hand, in Brittany an owl seen at harvest time means that there will be a good yield. In Germany if an owl hoots as a child is born, the infant will experience an unhappy life. In Ireland if an owl enters the house it must be killed or it will take the luck of the house with it when it leaves. And in Spain there is a legend that the owl used to sing sweetly until it saw Jesus die on the cross, after which it would only cry *cruz cruz* (cross cross).

If a careful, country-by-country survey were to be made, this list of surviving owl superstitions would undoubtedly fill many pages. Of course European city-dwellers would laugh at them, but country folk will have heard one or another of them, even today. Most will scoff at them and laugh at the suggestion that they have any basis in fact but even if they are only regarded as fanciful nonsense their retelling keeps them alive as part of local folklore.

Europe may have relegated many of its old myths and legends to the level of mere fairy tales, but in other parts of the world, stories about owls continue to be taken seriously and nowhere is this more true than on the still largely tribal continent of Africa.

AFRICAN OWLS

Owls do not fare well in the mythology of African tribes, where they are generally believed to be evil. In many places they are associated with witchcraft and killed whenever possible. The standard pidgin English name for the owl in West Africa is Witchbird. In parts of Cameroon the owl is considered to be so evil that it is forbidden to give it a name and it is known there only as the bird that makes you afraid. There, and also in parts of Nigeria, witches are reputed to transform themselves into owls at night.

In Zimbabwe it is the barn owl that is said to be the Witch's Bird. When asked why this species in particular was singled out a local ornithologist replied 'because it is white'. They are

considered to be bad luck and are killed whenever possible. Local witch doctors then use their beaks and claws to make powerful medicines that they use to cause harm. In Namibia the Balozi tribe believe that, simply by their presence, owls bring disease. As a result whenever owls enter a village they are shot. The Kikuyu in Kenya believe that, if an owl appears a death will follow.

This negative attitude to owls in Africa has played havoc with Western attempts to conserve some of the rare species, such as the Congo Bay owl. Culturally naïve conservationists who fail to understand local superstitions have little chance of introducing effective protection measures for these endangered birds.

The ability of the owl to see in the dark has, however, impressed African medicine men sufficiently for them to recommend eating owls' eyes to improve the night vision of human hunters or warriors.

Among the Kuba, a tribe from the Democratic Republic of Congo, status is displayed by the kind of hat worn on special occasions. Hats worn by the tribal chiefs are decorated with feathers. The highest official is the Eagle Feather Chief because eagles are considered to be the most powerful birds in the daytime sky. Next to him in importance comes the Chief of the Initiation Society, who wears an owl feather because owls are thought to be the rulers of the forest and the night sky. The Kuba also make expressive owl masks, depicting the birds with huge eyes, a sharp pointed beak and short, pricked ear-tufts.

The Songye tribe of the Congo also carve dramatic owl masks for special ceremonies. Theirs are usually painted a vivid black and white, with an oddly upturned mouth. They are very heavy to wear and the visibility from them is minimal, the

Owl with Child, carved by an artist of the Chockwe tribe, Angola. 20th century, wood. The Chokwe consider the owl to be a wise creature that has great knowledge acquired in the wild. This figure symbolizes how the ancestral spirits offer protection to future generations.

African *Kifwebe* owl mask, by an artist of the Songye tribe, Congo.

dancer's vision being restricted to what he can see from two narrow slits just below the large, rounded owl-eyes.

Among the Chockwe of Angola the owl is considered a wise creature that has great knowledge acquired in the wild. Ancestral figures are sometimes shown with a human body and the head of an owl, and are depicted in a protective role, caring for future generations.

ASIAN OWLS

In Asia, as in so many regions, there are good owls and bad owls. A common Asian myth is that owls eat newborn babies or hurt children. This belief is strongest in Malaysia, where owls are known as *burung hantu*, meaning ghost bird. In China and Korea there is a more practical approach towards owls. There they are killed and their parts are used in medical preparations. Further north, in Mongolia, it is thought that owls will enter the home during the night to gather human fingernails. Whether this is a case of good owls cleaning up the house or bad ones stealing away a small part of the nail-owners' souls is not clear. Those who are concerned with Mongolian burial rituals are known to hang up owl skins to ward off evil, but whether this is because the owl parts concerned possess good spirits that fend off the evil ones, or a case of evil repelling evil, is again not certain.

On the good side, in some parts of Asia owls have been honoured as divine ancestors and have been attributed with helping to avert famine and pestilence. On the island of Sulawesi (better known as Celebes) in Indonesia, some inhabitants claim that owls are so wise that they must always be consulted when a journey is being contemplated. If someone wants to travel they first listen to the owls. The birds make two different sounds at night; one says travel and the other says stay at home. These warnings are taken seriously. No journeys are undertaken if the owls give the stay-at-home cry.

AUSTRALIAN OWLS

Among the Australian Aborigines the owl does not hold an important place in tribal mythology but when it is mentioned it creates, yet again, the usual contradiction between the bad owl and the good owl. In its wicked form it is the messenger of the evil god Muurup, who eats children and kills people. And there is the familiar superstition, found in so many parts of the world, that if an owl hangs around the home site for a few days it means that someone is going to die. On the good side, there is a belief that owls represent the souls of women, or that they guard their souls. Women are therefore asked to protect owls as a way of protecting their female kin. Some authorities go so far as to say that this makes the owl a sacred bird, because 'your sister is an Owl – and the Owl is your sister'. (The souls of men, incidentally, are represented by bats.)

AMERICAN INDIAN OWLS

We are all aware of the popular image of a gigantic totem pole bearing the carved face of a severe owl that stares angrily down at us, but what precisely is the relationship between the tribes of North America and this nocturnal, predatory bird? Many of the tribes have complicated legends concerning supernatural owls and frequently these birds are associated with death, but not necessarily in a negative way. They are more likely to appear as helpful assistants in the process of making fruitful connections between the living and the dead. Native American tribes

Totemic owl: a
Pacific Northwest
coast totem pole.

often have shamans, or medicine men, whose tasks include communicating with the dead and they may enlist the owls to aid them in this. Indeed, the owl is sometimes referred to as the Bird of Sorcerers.

To give a specific example, in the Pima tribe a feather moulted by a living owl is placed in the hand of a dying person so that the owl will be able to guide that individual on the long journey to the afterlife. In other tribes owl feathers are also often used as magic talismans. Among the Navajo, following death the human soul actually assumes the form of an owl. The same is true of the Tsimshian people of the Pacific Northwest coast. In one of their imaginative dances a male performer is thrown into

A heart-shaped charm of painted wood: when opened it reveals an owl representing the soul of one who has recently died. Pacific Northwest coast.

a fire where his body appears to be consumed by the flames. Following this clever illusion, he emerges wearing a skull-like mask, but with his heart displayed intact. This heart, in the form of a carved wooden box, had been cunningly concealed in his clothing during the dance and is now magically revealed and opened to show a small owl, representing his surviving soul, sitting inside it.[1]

Because Native American tribes visualized such a strong link between owls and death it was inevitable that this would create ambivalent attitudes towards these birds. One tribe would see the owls as providers of helpful warnings about death, whereas another would see them as evil messengers who actually caused death. So, starting from the same premise, one tribe would come to respect owls while another would end up hating them. Those tribes that respected the owl included the Pawnee, who saw it as a symbol of protection; the Yakama, for whom it was a respected totemic figure; the Yupik, who wore ceremonial owl masks on special occasions and where owls were said to be helpful spirits; the Cherokee, who saw the owls as helpful consultants for the shaman, bringing prophetic news; the Lenape, who believed that if you dreamed of an owl it would become your guardian; the Tlingit, who claimed that owls would warn them of impending danger, and whose warriors hooted like owls when they went into battle, because they had faith that the owl would give them victory; the Oglala, whose warriors wore caps of snowy owl feathers to indicate their bravery; the Sioux, who believed that a man wearing owl feathers would have stronger, sharper vision; the Zuni, who placed an owl feather next to a baby to help it sleep; the Lakota, whose medicine men wore owl feathers and promised never to harm an owl in case they lost their magical powers; the Mohave, who became reincarnated as owls when they died; and the Kwakiutl,

The Wise Messenger Owl from the legend of Kwakwaka'wakw; 20th century, red cedar wood carving with cedar rope and bark tufts, by Wally Bernard, North Vancouver Island.

who owned owl-masks and who believed that each human is connected with a particular owl and that if someone killed your owl-half you too would die.

Those tribes that disliked owls include the Hopi, for whom the owl was a harbinger of ill fortune; the Apache, who feared owls and said that if you dreamed about one of these birds it was a sign of approaching death; the Cajun, who believed that if they were awoken by the cries of an owl, this was an ill omen; the Ojibway, who saw the owl as a symbol of evil and death; and the Caddo, the Catawba, the Choctaw, the Creek, the Menomini and the Seminole who all looked upon the owl as a bad omen and a sign of imminent death, often associated with witches.

Kuna Indian artist, 'Five Owls', late 20th century, reverse appliqué needlework, San Blas Islands, Panama.

101

Yet again the contradictory nature of the owl is evident. Because it was active at night and made strange, eerie noises, it became a ghostly bird and from there, in the hands of expert tribal storytellers, it soon became exaggerated into a benign and friendly ghost or a wicked, harmful one. Which kind of symbolic owl you met as a child and grew to know more intimately as an adult depended simply on which tribe you happened to be born into. But one thing is certain – it was rare for a North American Indian to know no spirit owl at all.

To find New World tribal owls that are portrayed simply for their own sake, as attractive birds without any haunting messages, we have to move south to the Central American country of Panama. There, among the Kuna Indians who inhabit the small islands of the San Blas Archipelago off the northern coast, there is a fascination with birds of many kinds, including the local owls. Images of the owls, and many other animals besides, appear on the clothing of the women who, unlike their male counterparts, have stubbornly retained the traditional costumes of their tribe, even in modern times. They wear decorative chest panels on their dresses, called *molas*. These are laboriously created by a process of reverse appliqué. It takes about 250 hours of meticulous needlework to complete a good example of one of these *molas* and they have recently become collected as serious works of tribal art.

There are fifteen kinds of owls living in Panama, but none of them has whiskers like a cat. But whenever a Kuna artist shows a face in front view there seems to be an overpowering urge to bewhisker it. There are cat-faced humans as well as cat-faced birds and it does not always stop at whiskers. With these owls the sharp-pointed beak of nature has become a blunt-ended nose, the eyes have grown eyelashes (or perhaps eyebrows) and the mouth has widened and grown teeth and conspicuous lips.

In fact these are feline-humanoid-owls with an endearingly primitive character all their own – one of the most charming inventions of the Kuna artists. The fact that they have protruding ear-tufts suggests that the real species on which they are based is the horned owl. Just for once these are owls employed for some visual fun, without the heavy burdens of legend, myth or symbolism to weigh them down.

On the rainforest mainland of Panama, in the Darien region not far from the Kuna, live another small group of surviving indigenous people, the Wounaan Indians. Their special skill is basket-weaving, an art-form the women of this tribe have been

Wounaan Indian owl mask of woven palm-frond fibre, a modern mask from Panama.

Wounaan Indian cloth appliqué *molita*: 'Owl on a branch'.

refining for hundreds of years. As with the Kuna, their tribal works of art have recently become known to the outside world and are now collectors' items. Occasionally the Wounaan also employ this skill to make masks and, when they do, a horned owl is one of their subjects. Each mask they create is made up of thousands of precise stitches, with intricate colour patterns. The making of one of these works of art involves five separate stages. First, locating, identifying and cutting the palm fronds from which the fibres will be made. This has to be done at the right time of year and using only two species of palm, the Black Palm and the Navala Palm. Second, drying, bleaching and stripping the fronds to obtain the individual fibres. Third, collecting the plant dyes with which to colour the fibres and then dying and redrying the fronds. Fourth, working out the complex design of the mask. Finally, stitching the fibres together to make the finished work, a process that by itself may take several weeks.

A less arduous creative process enjoyed by the Wounaan women is the making of small cloth appliqué patches called *molitas*. On these too the owl is a favoured subject. As with the Kuna, the Wounaan seem to employ owls simply as design motifs rather than as mythological or symbolic statements. This may explain why the Wounaan owls, like the Kuna ones, with all thoughts of witchcraft and sorcery swept away, are more decorative and warmly appealing than many of the owl images from other tribal cultures.

ESKIMO OWLS

Although technically another group of North American Indians, the Eskimo deserve separate treatment if only because owls appear more frequently in their art than in the work of any other ethnic group today. The best known of the Eskimo artists is Kenojuak Ashevak, and one of her owl stonecuts has become

Kenojuak Ashevak, *The Enchanted Owl*, 1971, stonecut print.

Kenojuak Ashevak, *Eskimo Spirit Owl*, 1971, stonecut print.

so famous that in 1970 Canada Post placed her 1960 print *The Enchanted Owl* on a 6 cent stamp to commemorate the centennial of the Northwest Territories. In this composition the way in which Kenojuak exaggerates the owl's plumage to create an unforgettable image is remarkable. When asked about her decision to modify the owl in this way, she replied that it was done to 'drive away the darkness'.

Over the years the owl has appeared many times in Kenojuak's pictures. In a monograph about her work, the image of an owl appears in no fewer than 89 of the 161 prints illustrated.[2] Sometimes she refers to it as a 'Spirit Bird' and may combine it with other birds such as gulls. When she does this, however, the owl remains the central feature, with the heads of the other birds growing out of the owl's feathers. In one of her Spirit Owls she adorns the bird with a forked fish-tail, emerging from behind the owl's head. In another work the image is called a 'Sun Owl'. Here the bird's rounded head becomes the sun and its radiating feathers become the rays of the sun. This association

Kenojuak Ashevak, *Sun Owl*, 1979, lithograph.

Iyola Kingwatsiak, *Three Owls*, 1966, etching.

106

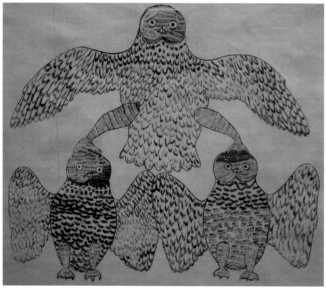

between the owl and the sun must be unique in owl symbolism. It is, of course, the result of the fact that the owl encountered by the Eskimo artist is the snowy owl, a daytime hunter that, unlike other owl species, is not averse to sunlight. Anyone who has visited the Arctic Circle will understand that, for the Eskimo, 'The arrival of the sun in the Arctic is a thing wonderful to behold',[3] and this means that by associating the owl with the sun Kenojuak has elevated this bird to the level of the wonderful.

Born in an igloo in 1927, Kenojuak has lived long enough to see her work honoured in her home country, where she was inducted into Canada's Walk of Fame in 2001. In 2004 she created the first ever Eskimo-designed stained glass window and this can now be seen in the John Bell Chapel at Appleby College in Oakville, Ontario. In 1964 a documentary film about her work was nominated for an Oscar.

Lucy, an older Eskimo artist born in 1915, has also created some memorable owls, her liveliest one being her 'Dancing Bird' of 1967. Much stiffer, more restrained owls are portrayed by a male Eskimo artist, Iyola Kingwatsiak (1933–2000), whose 1966 work 'Three Owls' strangely shows one bird clasping the heads of two others, one in each foot.

If owls seem unduly important to tribal peoples all over the world, this should not surprise us. For tribes live in small settlements, where owls will be encountered more freely than in towns or cities. Their cries will be more often heard and their silent shapes, hovering and floating through the dusk will be glimpsed far more frequently. The harsh mechanical sounds and the glaring artificial lights of the noisy urban centres mean that owls, once a spooky neighbour, are now more likely to become a rare and distant memory.

8 Owls and Artists

There must be more paintings of owls than of any other bird. It is such an easy shape to make that everyone feels the urge to draw, paint, model or sculpt one. There are sentimental owls, cartoon owls, kitsch owls, twee owls and comic owls. In addition to drawings, paintings and figures, the image of the owl appears repeatedly on household objects and whole books have been written on owls as collectables.

In modern times the owl has suffered the indignity of becoming the knick-knack bird. There are owl key-rings, owl paperweights, owl oven-gloves, owl bottle-openers, owl money-boxes, owl ashtrays, owl playing cards, owl feeding-bottles, owl teapots, owl inkstands, and on and on through almost every kind of ornamental object you can imagine. Owls have also appeared on banknotes, coins, medals, phone cards, matchbox labels and countless posters and advertisements. With the new craze for tattooing, owls have even managed to alight permanently on human skin.

In the realm of philately owls are everywhere. New Zealander Mike Duggan, whose obsession with acquiring every known postage stamp bearing the image of an owl has led to a huge collection, is currently offering for sale no fewer than 1,224 different owl stamps from 192 countries across the globe. Most nations have only produced a few owl stamps but some seem to

Owl postage stamps from the USA and the Marshall Islands.

Owl tattoo by Claudia of Frith Street Tattoo, London, on Linsay Trerise's arm.

have a special weakness for this particular subject. Angola has issued at least 30; Ivory Coast 32; Guinea Bissau 33; Benin 43 and Congo 44.

The obsession with collecting owl artefacts sometimes gets out of hand. In 1978 Monika Kirk was on holiday in Greece and bought a small owl pendant as a souvenir. Thirty years later she has no fewer than 1,950 owls making up the 'owl world' (*Eulenwelt*) displayed in her house, including 250 examples of owl jewellery: lockets, brooches, rings, ear-drops and earrings.

Despite their undeniable appeal, owl collectables are usually, at best, modest works of art. There are a few exceptions to

Owl with Spread Wings, 20th century, brass, by a local artist of Aqaba, Jordan.

Part of Monika Kirk's *Eulenwelt*, a collection of 1,950 owl artefacts.

this rule, however. From time to time, a master artist has been attracted to the owl image and has left us with an exceptional work. Great names that have given us owls to remember include Bosch, Dürer, Michelangelo, Goya and Picasso.

HIERONYMUS BOSCH (1450–1516)

Hieronymus Bosch, arguably the most darkly imaginative of all the Western masters, employed the image of the owl repeatedly in his work and nearly always gave it some kind of symbolic significance. One of the earliest of his owls is to be seen peering out of a niche above a door in *Gluttony*, one of the scenes from *The Seven Deadly Sins* that he completed in the 1470s or 1480s. The bird looks soberly down upon a scene of excessive human greed and drunkenness. According to a French art historian, this 'staring owl [is] a symbol of those who prefer the darkness of sin and heresy to the light of faith.'[1]

In another early work he employs the same device, an owl staring down at a scene of human debauchery and disarray. In

The Ship of Fools he shows us a monk and two nuns enjoying some drunken fun and games with a group of peasants. The mast of their little boat sprouts out into a tree in the branches of which sits the solemn owl, again apparently a nocturnal symbol of dark wickedness. One critic sees this curious mast as a Bosch metaphor for the Tree of Life, in which 'the staring owl, the bird of darkness, takes the place of the wily serpent' – another nocturnal predator.[2]

In *The Conjuror* Bosch's placing of an owl is truly bizarre. This bird, clearly a barn owl, appears as no more than a head

Owl nesting in the Fountain of Life in 'The Garden of Eden' of Bosch's triptych *The Garden of Earthly Delights*, 1503–4, oil on panel.

Hieronymus Bosch, *The Conjuror*, late 15th century, oil on wood.

113

Cuddled owl standing in water, in 'The Earthly Paradise', the centre panel of Bosch's *Garden of Earthly Delights*.

peeping out of a small basket hanging from the belt of the magician. The man is seen in the act of performing a trick for a rapt audience and the artist offers no explanation of the mysterious presence of the owl, or why it does not simply fly away, since the basket has an open top. It is hard to guess what possible trick the magician will do next that might involve a tame owl. Its presence has therefore again been seen as purely symbolic by art historians making a close study of this painting. They do not all agree, however, on the nature of this symbolism. Some see it as a sexual symbolism, with the spherical basket representing

Owl in an orange grove in 'The Earthly Paradise'.

the magician's genitals. For them: 'The bird of wisdom has thus taken the place of the seminal forces, which had to be removed to make room for it.'[3] Others see the owl as symbolizing the evil trickery of the conjuror/magician who is in the act of leading astray the foolish, gullible public, who are taken in by his tricks. For them, 'The frog on the table, the owl half-hidden in the basket, the dog with the clown's hat, are the symbolic expressions of credulity, heresy, the vile and ridiculous aspect of demonic power . . .'.[4]

In Bosch's major work, the great triptych called *The Millennium* but better known today as *The Garden of Earthly Delights*, several more owls put in an appearance. In the left-hand panel, *The Garden of Eden*, a pop-eyed owl stares out of a dark, circular hole in the fountain of life. According to one scholar, in this instance, 'the ultimate meaning of the owl is that its wisdom is grounded in the knowledge and transcendence of death.' This explains the position of the bird 'at the dead centre of the base of the fountain of life, where, from the omni-present, all-seeing, all-vivifying pupil of God's eye, the owl stares out at us – symbol of *Sophia* (= wisdom).'[5] Other authors see this owl in a totally different light. In fact they see all Bosch's owls as 'favourite symbols of death' or 'evil lurking symbols of witch-craft and demonology' because this was the predominant view of the bird in the medieval period when Bosch was working.[6] Once again we are faced with the contradiction that sees the owl both as a wise old bird and as an evil spirit of the night. And if learned scholars who have spent a lifetime studying the complex imagery of Bosch's work cannot agree, then it is clear that, in truth, the artist has left us with an insoluble problem.

In the great central panel of the triptych there are several more owls and it has to be said that, if they are supposed to be symbols of evil, they are remarkably friendly and cuddly-looking birds. Indeed, the large one standing in shallow water on the extreme left of the panel is actually being cuddled by a small naked human, whose left hand is gently embracing the bird's breast. One scholar interprets this as depicting 'a young boy who has entrusted himself to an owl as a sign that he has given himself over to the hallowed wisdom of nature, like his companions, who unconcernedly snuggle up to their feathered teachers.'[7] This does seem a more appropriate interpretation of a scene that is supposed to be depicting 'earthly delights'. Unless, of course, Bosch was extolling the view of the sour medieval churchmen who saw all forms of pleasure as wicked and all forms of wisdom as a threat to the ignorant innocence of the true believer.

ALBRECHT DÜRER (1471–1528)

Albrecht Dürer, the greatest Renaissance artist of northern Europe, is another matter altogether. He was clearly fascinated by owls and his watercolour sketch of an owl dated 1508 has become the most famous and best loved image of an owl in the history of art. Born in Nuremberg, Dürer travelled a great deal around Europe and made copious notes of the wild fauna he encountered on his journeys. His amazingly accurate and life-like portraits of these animals, often filling the page to the exclusion of any human imagery, make him virtually the first serious wildlife artist in the history of Western art. Dürer's owl is an owl as an owl – an objective zoological portrayal without any of the usual symbolic overtones. This owl was neither good nor evil, it simply sat for its portrait and was faithfully recorded, creating a work of art that was 500 years ahead of its time.

This does not mean that Dürer was immune to the prevailing urge to render owls as symbolic images. In a number of

1508

works he showed the owl being mobbed by other birds. In one such work this mobbing takes place just above the head of a sad looking Christ. The interpretation of this work is that 'The owl will share the same fate as the wisest of men, besieged by jealous birds just as Christ was killed by men deaf to his words.'[8] This interpretation, which sees the mobbed owl as a symbol of a mobbed Christ just before his crucifixion, is at odds with other early readings of this avian event, where the mobbed owl in its wicked persona is viewed as 'evil attacked by the forces of good', or the creature of the night attacked by the 'enlightened' birds of the daytime. Perhaps Dürer, the avid naturalist, was too fond of owls to portray them in a derogatory fashion.

MICHELANGELO (1475–1564)

The divine Michelangelo, as he was known in his own lifetime, was primarily occupied with the human form and rarely depicted animals unless, like horses or domestic livestock, they happened to be associated with a human figure. He only produced a single sculpture of an owl and even that had to play a supporting role to a reclining female nude. The nude in question represented 'Night' and the owl was there to act as a symbol of nocturnal darkness. It stands beneath the raised left leg of the woman, with its feet planted firmly on the ground. It is a proud, powerful bird with muscular thighs and a puffed out chest. Its face suggests that it is based on a barn owl. This single owl sculpture by Michelangelo is to be seen in the Church of San Lorenzo in Florence, where it is part of a major work that included the tomb of Giuliano de' Medici. Work on this tomb began in 1526 and was completed in 1531 and features two nudes, 'Night' (a woman) and 'Day' (a man). These figures symbolize human life as being subject to the laws of time and the

Little Owl by Albrecht Dürer, 1508, watercolour.

Michelangelo's owl, a detail of his tomb for Giuliano de' Medici, 1526–31, San Lorenzo, Florence.

passing of days. The presence of the sculpted owl acts as a label announcing 'this figure is the one that represents the night-time'. Some art historians have tried to make more of the owl's presence, commenting that there is something protective about it. Its position, standing defiantly under the bent knee of the woman's leg, closes off the space that would otherwise give access to her genital region, almost as if the bird is standing guard over her more private parts. Could this therefore also be showing the owl in its protective role? Or is it the owl in its more sinister role, associated with death? In which case, perhaps the artist is playing with the idea of placing a symbol of death right next to the part of the woman's body that produces life. It is insoluble arguments of this kind that keep art historians endlessly at one another's throats.

During his lifetime Michelangelo hardly ever depicted any sort of animal wildlife. Even the painting of the snake in the Garden of Eden that appears on the roof of the Sistine Chapel is a humanoid creature with a man's head, arms and torso and only the tail of a serpent. Among his graphic work, there are two drawings of an eagle engaged in mortal combat with a human figure and one of a lion in a similar context. There is a rough sketch of a dragon or two and a tiny scribble of a giraffe, and that it is. The owl is the only wild animal that he ever created as a sculptural form, a singular honour for this singular bird.[9] Michelangelo's rival Leonardo da Vinci (1452–1519), who was much more interested in depicting a whole variety of animal forms, from the crab and dragonfly to the bear and wolf, apparently never fashioned an owl. His birds were limited to the eagle, falcon, duck and parrot.

FRANCISCO GOYA (1746–1828)

In the eighteenth century the Spanish master Francisco Goya viewed the owl as a nocturnal monster, a creature of nightmares waiting to attack. In his famous etching from the *Caprichos* cycle he depicts an artist (presumably himself) slumped asleep over his work-table. Around him swirl more than a dozen sinister-looking winged animals. The ones in the distance appear to be giant bats, but when they come closer and we see them more clearly in the light of the room, they have the wings and faces of owls. These owl-bats, or bat-owls, are clearly meant to be haunting the dreams of the sleeper, assailing him from all sides and about to strike him. Here and

El sueño de la razon produce monstruos

Goya, 'Is there no one left to untie us?', etching and aquatint.

elsewhere in Goya's etchings we meet again the evil owl that emerges from the darkness to do us harm.

In Goya's series *The Disasters of War*, full of unforgettable scenes of rape, torture and death, the owl also puts in a dramatic appearance, although its symbolic role here is slightly different.[10] The artist created this series as a personal reaction to the atrocities committed in the Peninsular War (1808–14). The earlier plates show specific incidents of brutality but the later ones are more allegorical. One, with the curious title of *Feline Pantomime*, shows a religious congregation worshipping

Francisco Goya, *The Sleep of Reason Produces Monsters*, 1797–9, etching and aquatint.

a large cat, in the manner of the ancient Egyptians at Bubastis. Down swoops a huge owl, clearly intent on sinking its claws into the cat, which twists its head slightly in anticipation of the assault. It would seem that here Goya is making a veiled attack on the Church and has enlisted the owl as a destroyer of false idols. So although this owl is a killer, depicted in a moment of impending savagery, its function here is to oppose and destroy the object of worship of a misguided priesthood. Seen alongside Goya's other, nightmare owls, this one confirms the artist's use of the owl as a general symbol of death and destruction, even though the subjects under attack may vary.

EDWARD LEAR (1812–1888)

Edward Lear was a serious Victorian artist whose landscapes and animal paintings have been overshadowed by the nonsense verse and cartoons that he created to amuse the children of his patron, the Earl of Derby. Lear was an ambitious artist, who at one point was engaged to teach Queen Victoria how to draw, but whose output suffered from the fact that he was a slave to epileptic fits and to periods of acute depression. Had he not been cursed by ill health all his life, we might well know him today as a major artist. A close examination of his owl paintings reveals the extraordinary quality of his work. One of his most striking owl portraits is of a spectacled owl, painted in 1836 when he was in his early twenties.[11]

PABLO PICASSO (1881–1973)

Edward Lear,
Spectacled Owl,
1836, watercolour.

Because of its distinctive head shape and large eyes, the owl has remained a favourite image among artists today. Pablo Picasso produced a whole series of owl paintings and drawings in the

124

1940s and '50s and, when he turned his hand to ceramics, the owl was a frequent subject for jugs and jars. He even thought of himself as an owl because of his famously staring eyes. On one occasion, when his friend the photographer David Duncan Douglas had taken a close-up of his intense stare, he turned them into the eyes of an owl. Duncan made two enlargements and asked Picasso to sign them for him. The artist refused 'then picked up his sketch pad, tore out two pages, reached for his scissors, then his charcoal, and in a couple of minutes finished two self-portraits of Pablo Picasso as an owl.' He did this in each case by cutting out just his two eyes from the photograph, glueing them to the sketch-pad page and then drawing the head of an owl around them.[12]

Pablo Picasso, *The Owl*, 1953, painted terracotta.

Picasso examining his self-portrait as an owl, photographed by David Duncan Douglas.

126

Picasso with an owl.

Picasso was fascinated by owls and was well aware of the fact that his own face had an owl-like quality. On one occasion he even kept a live little owl in his house as a pet. It had been given to him at Antibes by the portrait photographer Michel Sima (1912–1987) in 1946, who took a memorable photograph of Picasso holding the bird. Sima had found the owl in the corner of the Musée d'Antibes, where Picasso was working. It was in a sad state, one of its claws having been injured, and Picasso took it under his care and had the claw bandaged until it had healed. The owl was placed in a special cage and taken to Paris, where it lived in Picasso's kitchen, alongside his canaries, pigeons and doves. He fed it on mice, trapped in his studio where they were apparently plentiful, but it proved to be rather a sullen pet, offering its new owner no more than an occasional snort. When this happened, Picasso would shout obscenities at the owl, but they had no effect, except to produce yet another snort.

Picasso's little owl was a very private bird, refusing to eat a proffered mouse while anyone was in the kitchen. If the room was vacated for only a minute, however, the mouse had vanished when the artist returned. In her autobiography *Life with Picasso* Françoise Gilot recorded that Picasso 'used to stick his fingers between the bars of the cage and the owl would bite him, but Pablo's fingers, though small, were tough and the owl didn't hurt him. Finally the owl would let him scratch his head and gradually he came to perch on his finger instead of biting it, but even so, he still looked very unhappy.' Picasso used his pet as a model for his 1946 painting of an owl perched on the top of a chair, called *Owl on a Chair and Sea Urchins*, and there is a later photograph of him

Pablo Picasso,
The Owl Cage,
1947, oil on panel.

holding the now rather unhappy owl in his hands, with the painting placed behind them. This photograph therefore has three pairs of intensely staring eyes – his, the bird's and the painting's, and the similarity between the three was obviously his intention in creating what must have been a difficult pose to hold.[13]

Pablo Picasso,
*Owl on a Chair and
Sea-urchins*, 1946,
oil on wood.

When it came to owl symbolism, although Picasso must have known that these birds were a symbol of wisdom in

ancient Greece, he himself saw them more as monsters of the night, heralding death. He must have been aware of Goya's etching *The Sleep of Reason Produces Monsters*, discussed earlier, with its sleeping human figure surrounded by a flock of sinister-looking owls. And in 1948 Picasso made a sinister sketch of a disembowelled horse (an image taken from his knowledge of the way horses were abused in Spanish bullfights) which is shown with an owl sitting quietly on its head – clearly a symbol of the impending death of the wounded animal.

RENÉ MAGRITTE (1898–1967)

Owls appear several times in the work of Belgian surrealist René Magritte. Their first portrayal is in a sombre work from 1942, called *The Companions of Fear*. Painted in Brussels during the Nazi occupation of Belgium it depicts a desolate, rocky landscape in which plants are stubbornly breaking through the hard surface. Five of these plants have blossomed, not into flowers, but into green owls. The leaves, as they rise up vertically from the ground, are gradually transformed into the bodies of the owls, creating a leaf/bird hybrid. The image, as in much of Magritte's work, is disturbing because it plays tricks with one's mind. In a letter to a friend, written some years before, the artist commented: 'I have made a really striking discovery in painting. Up to now . . . the position of an object was sometimes enough to make it mysterious. But as a result of the experiments I've made here, I have found a new potential in things – their ability to become gradually something else, an object merging into an object other than itself . . . By this means I produce pictures which the eye must "think" in a completely different way from the usual one.'[14]

The leaf-owls in this painting have a sinister quality. These are not wise or friendly owls, they are killers. It is as though

Owls growing as plants: René Magritte, *The Companions of Fear*, 1942, gouache on paper.

Magritte is saying that during the wartime Nazi occupation, when fear pervaded the whole country, even the vegetation is liable to transform itself into a group of stealthy nocturnal predators. In 1944 he painted a similar scene, but here the owls have turned white. The central bird has huge ear-tufts that look like horns and Magritte writes to a friend about the 'pair of pointed ears in my pictures . . . Could there be a relationship with satanism?'[15] In other words, he is thinking of owls in their evil, satanic role.

As World War II raged on Magritte decided to react against the drab misery of the period by introducing a new style of painting, called his 'sunshine' works, in which he adopted a defiantly optimistic, cheerful approach to his imagery and employed an impressionist technique. In one of these paintings, called *The Sleepwalker*, he shows us a large owl sitting in a sunlit window. The bird is relaxing with a drink and is contentedly smoking a pipe. A Magritte authority comments: 'What is significant is that even a lover of darkness and night, the owl, is seen to revel in the presence of light and sunshine. For all its sentimentalism, this work is a fusion of irreconcilables – light and the tenebrous owl. It is the realization of the impossible, a sunshine-loving nocturnal predator.'[16] With his typical perversity, Magritte has shown us the bird of darkness enjoying the bright light of day, something a real owl never does. The political message is clear. To the Nazis he is saying, you may have brought us dark days but you cannot crush our spirit. Just the opposite in fact – even the creature that is synonymous with the dark has come out into the sunlight.

OTHER MODERN ARTISTS

Paul Klee, Max Ernst, Salvador Dalí, Jacques Herold, Graham Sutherland, Bernard Buffet and numerous others have occasionally included the owl in their repertoire, but they have often failed to do the bird justice or create any memorable images of it. The American Morris Graves (1910–2001), however, who specialized in idiosyncratic bird paintings, did leave us one haunting image, which, if not specifically of an owl, was certainly inspired by one. Called *Little Known Bird of the Inner Eye*, it shows a strange, four-legged bird with a broad, flat face and a small, open beak, enclosed in a cramped cavity or cave. Like the hieroglyphic Egyptian owl, its body is seen in profile while its face is depicted staring head-on at the viewer. Painted in 1941, at the height of World War II, it has been said of this picture that: 'This owl-inspired image expresses the artist's idea of a hidden part of the mind in which we know a higher reality than that of the daily world.' Graves himself remarked that 'I paint to rest from the phenomena of the external world . . . and to make notations of its essences with which to verify the inner eye.'[17] It is as though this particular owl-like creature was hiding from the horrors of war by retreating into a safe space, hidden away from the chaos outside. Or, perhaps, that wisdom, in the symbolic shape of a quadrupedal owl, was in retreat from the brutish stupidity of mankind at war.

Self-taught artists known as Modern Primitives, Sunday painters or Outsider artists have from time to time produced an owl to remember. In England the wonderfully idiosyncratic artist Fred Aris (*b*. 1932), who used to run a café in south London but who now paints full time, has produced his own unique version of the famous Owl and the Pussycat. Far out at sea a huge ginger tabby lies in the prow of a small rowing boat while the owl sits stiffly erect in the stern, with a guitar strapped on its

Morris Graves, *Little Known Bird of the Inner Eye*, 1941, gouache.

Tom Duimstra ('tom d'), *Two Owls and Bird*, after 2000, acrylic and collage on cardboard.

back. Both these nocturnal predators look suitably despondent to find themselves in such an inappropriate environment, but they seem to have accepted their lot. It is too far for the cat to swim ashore and the owl cannot fly home because of the weight of the guitar, so there they sit, patiently fulfilling the demands of Mr Lear's nonsense verse.[18]

In the United States, the increasingly well-known Outsider artist Tom Duimstra (*b. c.* 1952), who always signs himself simply as 'tom d', has a special fondness for owls. Tom, who hails from Grand Rapids, Michigan, has become the favourite folk artist of many American celebrities, such as actress Susan Sarandon, singer Courtney Love and author Tom Robbins, who have started collecting his work. He has exhibited with Andy

The Owl House archway by Helen Martins at Nieu Bethesda, South Africa.

Warhol in Holland and his owls have a splendidly primitive quality. Once seen, they are hard to forget.

In South Africa an outsider art masterpiece exists at the remote village of Nieu Bethesda. Called *The Owl House* it represents a lifetime's labour of love on the part of an eccentric recluse by the name of Helen Martins (1897–1976). Helen was born in the village but left to become a teacher. Married and divorced, she returned to her birthplace in the late 1920s to care for her elderly parents. When they died she found herself, in her late forties, alone and isolated. Unpopular with the other residents she hid herself away more and more. To put some colour into her grey world, she decided to transform her Karoo house into a monumental work of art.

The house, its walls encrusted with crushed glass, luminous paint, multi-coloured panes and angled mirrors reflecting the many candles that burned there, created a world of fantasy. Outside, she surrounded the building with hundreds of strange models and large sculptured figures of mythical beasts. The arched entrance way from the street was watched over by a stoic, double-faced owl. The whole project became an obsession that continued until, at the age of 78, she killed herself by drinking caustic soda. Today, The Owl House is a tourist attraction open to visitors, who are startled by the surreal world she built there over many years, dominated by statues of huge owls with their wings spread wide, as if about to launch themselves down onto the human heads below. The house was declared a national monument in 1991.

Finally, the latest well-known figure to give us an interesting image of an owl is the notorious British artist Tracey Emin (*b.* 1963). Tracey, widely ridiculed for presenting her unmade bed to the Tate as an art exhibit, is a far more serious artist than the tabloids would have us believe. She is also, despite her infamously explicit presentation of her busy sex life, a complex individual whose celebrity lifestyle appears to be an attempt to conceal her true personality. It is in her small etching of an owl, however, that the truth, perhaps unintentionally, emerges. The clue is in the title: *Little Owl – Self-portrait.* The owl in question is shown to us very alone, sitting rather dishevelled and forlorn, in the crook of a tree. Apart from that, the scene is completely empty. In nature the owl is a solitary bird and Emin's owl is as lonely as they come. If this is how she sees herself, then she has yet to find the kind of fulfilment that one senses she craves. As with so many other artists, the owl to her is more than an owl, it is a symbol or metaphor of some sort, and here the message appears to be that the owl stands for being alone.

It would be possible to track down hundreds more works of art depicting owls. Clearly, for artists everywhere, owls are a visual gift. Even artists who rarely draw or paint other kinds of birds occasionally find it impossible to resist outlining those

Tracey Emin, *Little Owl – Self-portrait*, 2005, etching.

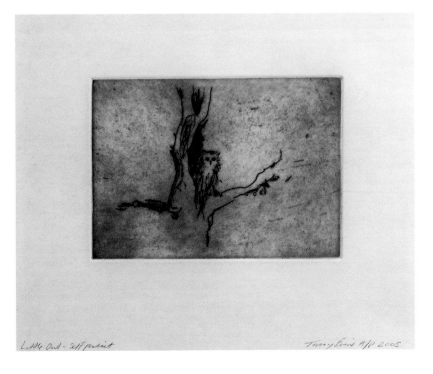

huge eyes and that wonderfully rounded head. Because of the rich mythological history of the owl image, it is tempting to seek a symbolic interpretation of every painted owl we see, but that would be a mistake. For many artists the owl is simply a beautiful shape to be relished for its own sake, with no legendary or deep psychological undertones. For some, symbolism may be important, but for others we may be better served ignoring the sometimes ludicrously convoluted interpretations of art historians and accept that, as Gertrude Stein might have said, an owl is an owl is an owl . . .

9 Typical Owls

Having examined all the many ways in which human beings have viewed or interacted with owls over the centuries, it remains to ask the question: what is the scientific truth about these remarkable birds? How many of the old tales about owls are based on reality and how many are wild distortions or romantic exaggerations? A great deal of research has been done on the owl family in recent years and we now have a clear picture of what makes a typical owl and how many unusual variations there are.

All owls are predators and the vast majority of owl species are active only at night. A few species, like the snowy owl that inhabits the cold Arctic regions, have however adapted to daytime hunting. Owls have wonderful vision, amazing hearing and a characteristic, broad-headed silhouette that makes them immediately recognizable. A owl is an owl and there are no half-measures. There are no intermediate forms that cause arguments as to whether a particular bird is, or is not, an owl.

The majority of owls have the great advantage, for a predator, of silent flight, although a few species have abandoned this feature and now have audible wing-beats like other birds. The typical owl also has a special foot design, called zygodactylous (literally, 'paired toes'), in which there are two claws pointing forward and two back. Most other birds have three claws

Snowy owl with feathered feet.

Owl camouflage: African Scops owl resting on a camelthorn tree in Namibia.

pointing forward and only one pointing back. In the snowy owl, the feet are well covered in feathers as a protection against the freezing ground.

Socially, owls are rather solitary beings, hiding away by themselves, sleeping during the day, and hunting alone at night. With a few exceptions, they only come together in the breeding season. Burrowing owls are the only ones that break this rule on a regular basis, and can often be observed near their burrows in little groups of several families together. Despite their solitary nature, the English language does have a collective name for owls. A group of them is referred to as a parliament of owls. Whether they acquired this name because they are thought to be wise or because there is a belief that they are wicked is not clear.

Some owls, if safe roosting places are scarce, may tolerate a few sleeping companions. Sleeping owls are vulnerable and their urge for privacy has to be weighed against their need for daytime security. If there happens to be a large and particularly attractive hollow tree in one spot and no other suitable roost anywhere near, a group of owls will use it together, not as an active social centre, but merely as a dormitory of convenience. If there are no suitable crevices for a sleeping owl, then it must make do with a high perch snug against a tree trunk. This is where the typical, speckled brown plumage of the owl becomes important, acting as camouflage against the bark of the tree. Some owls even manage to adopt a posture that makes them look like the extension of a tree stump, where they will remain motionless, with their eyes firmly closed and almost invisible to the casual passer-by.

The eyes of owls are remarkably big for their body size, the eyes of some species weighing as much as those of a human being. They also have a large exposed corneal surface, and are set wide apart. These are all special adaptations for life as a nocturnal bird of prey. The wide set of the eyes in the skull, the feature that gives these birds their characteristic, broad-headed silhouette, helps to improve their stereoscopic vision, so important in catching their prey. They do, in fact, have the best stereoscopic vision of all birds.

The frontally placed eyes of an owl are its most conspicuous feature, but an owl will never roll them at you or give you a side-long glance. This is because unlike human eyes those of an owl are fixed in their sockets. If an owl wants to look to one side it cannot turn its eyes but must turn its entire head. It is remark-ably efficient at this manoeuvre, being able to rotate its head through 270 degrees and tilt it up and down through 90 degrees. This is possible because it has fourteen neck vertebrae, twice as many as a human being, giving it its remarkable neck flexibility.

Most animals have spherical eyes, but owls do not. Instead of eyeballs they have tubular eyes. These remarkable eyes are held in place by bony sclerotic rings or scleral ossicles. It is this tubular shape that makes it impossible for the bird to rotate its eyes inside their sockets. It has sometimes been thought that this strange eye-shape has evolved as an aid to night vision, but the world's greatest authority on animal eyes, Gordon Walls, states categorically that it 'adds nothing to the capacity of the eye for operation in a dim light'.[1] What it does do, however, is to enable the owl family to evolve large eyes without taking up too much head-space. If owls had huge spherical eyeballs, there

A northern spotted owl with its head rotated to peer behind it.

144

would be little room left between them for their brains. The tubular shape of an owl's eyes is concealed from us when we look at the adult bird, but with some owl chicks this strange feature is clearly visible when they are only a few weeks old, giving them the appearance of an alien being from another planet.

Each eye possesses three eyelids, an upper, a lower and a nictitating one. The nictitating eyelid flashes diagonally across the eye's corneal surface, cleaning it or protecting it. The owl is able to use these semi-transparent third eyelids singly or in unison. Nearly all owl species have bright yellow irises, making a conspicuous contrast with the central black spot of the pupil. In some species this yellow colour darkens to orange, or even further to brown, but when the owls are active at night these colour differences are irrelevant because the pupils then expand to fill the entire space with black.

Grey owl with small pupils in bright light.

A four-week old Verraux's eagle owl chick, showing the strange, tubular shape of the owl's eye.

Close-up of orange owl eyes.

The owl's eyes have two key tasks – to see in very dim light and to pick out the tiniest movement on the ground. These two requirements – visual sensitivity and visual acuity – are crucial to the owl's survival as a nocturnal predator. It is no surprise therefore that they have excellent long-distance vision, although their ability to bring close-up objects into sharp focus is poor. Nor is it a surprise to learn that careful tests with barn owls proved that their visual sensitivity is at least 35 times better than that of humans.

One of the great misconceptions about owls is that they cannot see in bright light. This supposed weakness has been the basis for legends and folktales for centuries, but it is simply not true. In fact, the majestic eagle owl has slightly better daytime vision than human beings. The pupils of owls can close right down to pin-pricks, through which a greatly reduced amount of sunlight is allowed to penetrate, enabling them to see even at noon.

EARS

Even with its wonderfully precise long-distance vision an owl may not always be able to see its prey. Its intended victim may be hidden below a carpet of leaves, for example, and the only clue to its position then will be the faint rustling sound it makes. This is where the owl's highly sensitive hearing comes into play. Experiments with owls in the laboratory have shown that their sense of hearing is about ten times better than that of humans. Other tests have revealed that even in total darkness barn owls can detect and kill mice, providing that their victims are making some sort of rustling or squeaking noises.

It must be stressed that the conspicuous ear-tufts of some owl species, that protrude like a pair of horns from the top of

their heads, have nothing whatever to do with hearing. Their
primary role is as a signalling device, indicating either the mood
of an owl or the species to which it belongs. The true ears are
always completely hidden in the feathers at the sides of the owl's
broad head. If, with a tame owl, these feathers are spread gently
apart with the fingers, the extensive ear apertures beneath them
are revealed. The remarkably advanced development of the ears
of owls is not a new discovery. A diagram showing their complex structure beneath the head feathers was published as long
ago as 1646 in the great *Natural History* of Aldrovandus.

In their most advanced form the ears of an owl are placed
asymmetrically on the bird's head, with one ear being higher
than the other. The result of this is that minute sounds coming
up from the ground below will arrive at one ear a fraction of a

second earlier than at the other ear and so will be louder in one ear than the other. Also, if the prey is to the left of the spot where the bird is hovering, the sounds it makes as it rustles along through the foliage will reach the owl's left ear before the right one, and vice versa. Astonishingly, in receiving these sounds owls are capable of detecting time differences of as little as 30 millionths of a second. It is hardly surprising that the region of the bird's brain that is concerned with the reception of sounds is far more advanced in owls than in other birds. It is, for example, three times as complex as in the crow.

Aiding this refined hearing process is the possession in most owls of a concave facial disc of tiny feathers. This disc acts like a radar dish, guiding sounds into the ears, and there are even special facial muscles that can alter the concavity of the dish, making it deeper or shallower as the bird hovers above its prey, assessing its precise position. Once it is certain of the victim's location it makes its swift, silent swoop downwards, with its toes spread wide open ready to grasp the unsuspecting prey in a lethal grip. If the prey moves during this rapid descent the owl is capable of adjusting its flight path accordingly.

In the 1960s some tests were carried out to discover which owls had the best hearing. The results showed that those species living in northern forests had better hearing than those from the tropics. This makes sense when one thinks of what it must be like to hunt at night in a northern pine forest, compared with a tropical rain forest. Midnight in a cold northern forest must be as silent as the grave, where even a mouse's footstep could be heard by a hovering owl. Midnight in a tropical rain forest, on the other hand, with the night air filled with chirping insects and calling frogs, would be much too noisy for an owl to isolate a particular prey by its sounds alone. For tropical owls the half-light of dawn and dusk would inevitably become more important hunting times, when vision could play a bigger role in detecting their prey.

When out hunting at night the owl will hover for a while, watching and listening with its amazing eyes and ears. If it detects nothing, it will silently move on to a new spot and hover there. Once it has detected its prey it will swoop down until it is about 60 cm (2 feet) away and then swing its feet into a forward position with its toes spread out and its sharp claws poised for action. Then in a split second it pounces on its victim and clasps it tight, usually killing it instantly. If there is any resistance the powerful curved beak can be brought into play. At this point the owl usually flies off to a branch, carrying the corpse either in its claws or, if it is not too bulky, in its beak. Once it settles on the branch it proceeds to swallow its prey whole, usually taking several vigorous gulps to complete the process. Only on rare occasions when the victim happens to be unusually large will the owl start tearing it to pieces before swallowing it. Very small prey may sometimes be gobbled down without delay, right where they are caught.

Some species of owls have shorter wings than others and this type generally prefer what is called perch-hunting. They take up a suitable position on a post or perch of some kind and sit there quietly waiting for a victim to stir in their vicinity. When this happens, they swoop down immediately and pounce. This less energetic form of hunting demands an environment where the pickings are easy.

During the hunt it is important that the prey, who may also have sensitive ears, does not hear the owl coming. The eerie silence of the owl in flight has already been mentioned, but how

Owl with prey, from Ulysses Aldrovandus, *Ornithologia*, Book VIII, from *Opera Omnia* (1656).

this is achieved has not been explained. The secret is in the design of the flight feathers, the long primary pinions of the wings. In other birds these are stiff with a coarse surface and smooth edges, like the quill of a quill pen, but with owls they have delicately fringed, serrated edges and a soft velvety surface. These qualities decrease the sharpness of the air movement around the owl's wings as they beat in the night air and dampen the swishing sound that one might expect to hear as a bird hovers or flies by. There is a cost in this refinement, however,

A hunting barn owl hovering over a field.

because the softer wing feathers mean harder work for the hunting owl, but the huge advantage that silent flight brings to a stealthy predator makes the extra effort well worthwhile.

Pels fishing owl (*Scotopelia peli*) with catfish prey.

The diet of owls is varied but rodents in the shape of voles, mice and rats must account for the bulk of the food taken. In this respect the owls must be considered valuable pest-controllers and the farmers' friend. Sadly, the refusal of old superstitions about owls to die away has meant that even today, in some regions, owls are still persecuted instead of treasured.

Other foods taken include a variety of small birds and occasionally rabbits, fish, amphibians and reptiles. Bigger owls have no respect for their own kind and often prey on the smaller owl species. The largest of all owls have been known to prey on animals as big as foxes, small deer and dogs. The smallest prefer large insects, spiders and other invertebrates. Insects may be caught on the wing.

When food becomes unusually plentiful, owls have been known to stock up a small larder for themselves. The surplus kills may be pushed into a tree-hole, in the crease or fork of a suitable branch, or sometimes even in the nest.

PELLETS

Owls that swallow their prey whole are faced with a problem. They may avoid having to perform laborious food preparation sequences but as a result are left with a stomach full of indigestible material, such as bones, beaks, claws, teeth, scales and insect skeletons. This unwanted material is gathered into a wet, slimy oblong pellet and is then regurgitated by the bird. Regurgitation is helped by the fact that owls somehow manage to form the pellet in a special way, enclosing the sharper objects inside an outer layer of smoother rejected material such as fur

Preceding pages:
Barn owl (*Tito alba*) with prey.

Eagle owl (*Bubo bubo*) with dead rabbit.

Owl disgorging a pellet.

or feathers. The owl is then left with the soft parts of the prey that it can easily digest with the aid of proteolytic enzymes and stomach acids.

These pellets, found on the ground near an owl roost or nest, are of enormous help to ornithologists. By collecting them from the woodland or forest floor and carefully dissecting them and analysing their undigested contents, it is possible to assess with great accuracy the feeding habits of the owls. The investigators

Burrowing owl with newly disgorged pellet.

are helped in this by the fact that owls have a rather narrow pyloric opening from the stomach into the intestines. This prevents all but the tiniest bones or other fragments from passing onwards from the stomach, so that the regurgitated pellet usually contains virtually the complete skeletons of the prey animals devoured the night before, facilitating the identification of the prey species.

The analysis of owl pellets is such an excellent teaching device that there are even specialized companies set up solely to supply pellets to schools and other educational establishments. For example: *Pellets Inc.* boasts: 'We take pride in providing the best barn owl pellets and the most complete line of support products available in the world . . . Because we collect, heat sterilize, sort, wrap, and ship every pellet we sell, we guarantee the highest quality and service. For 18 years the same *Pellets Inc.*

employee has carefully hand-sorted and wrapped every pellet we sell.'[2]

The production of pellets by the owl follows a regular cycle. First, the owl hunts, kills and swallows its prey whole. The small corpse slides down the bird's oesophagus and, since owls have no crop, straight into its glandular stomach, the proventriculus, where it is attacked by the digestive juices. It then moves on to the muscular stomach, or gizzard, where the digestible parts of the prey are passed on to the intestines for absorption, while the indigestible parts are compacted into the pellet. This pellet is then passed back up into the glandular stomach where it is stored for up to ten hours. During this phase of the cycle the owl cannot feed because the pellet is blocking the system. When the owl is ready to hunt again, it starts to show discomfort. It

Contents of the pellet of a long-eared owl (*Asio otus*).

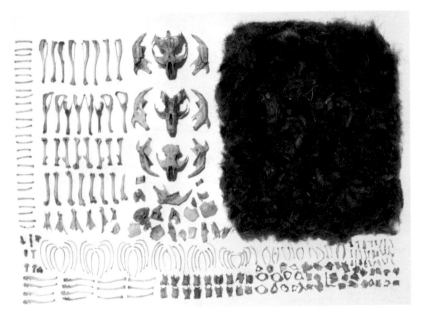

closes its eyes and stretches its neck upwards and forwards with its beak open. At this point the pellet drops out of its mouth and falls to the ground. Now the bird is ready to hunt once more and the cycle is complete.

It has been said that owls are more often heard than seen, which may explain why some people fear them and others find them eerie and unearthly. Songbirds they are not. Even the traditional *tu-whit tu-whoo* that tawny owls are supposed to call out is too friendly and too kind to them. To listen to most owls crying in the night air, you might imagine you were standing outside a torture chamber. It is said that they hoot but in reality they are more likely to shriek, scream, screech and squawk. Others are known to growl, snore, buzz, cough or chime. Some sound like machines that need oiling, others like a man trying to start a car with a flat battery. Still others sound like a giant grasshopper or a cross between a barking terrier and a gibbon. Only the biggest owls produce smoother, softer sounds and even these are reminiscent of someone pretending to be a ghost to frighten a small child.

Recordings of great horned owls (*Bubo virginianus*) are intriguing because they reveal that each bird has its own personal morse code of *woo-woos* which presumably means that individuals can easily identify one another even though they all have no more than two notes in their 'song', a long *woooo* and a short *woo*.

One will go: *woooo-woo-woo-woo-woooo-woooo*
While another calls: *woooo-woo-woo woo-woo-woooo*
And a third calls: *woooo-woo-woo-woo woooo-woooo-woooo*

These subtle differences will be enough for rival males, hooting to one another at night, to signal their territorial positions and to defend their hunting grounds. If one owl suddenly stops hooting at night, his territory will gradually be absorbed by neighbouring rivals.

In the breeding season, the hooting of the males will attract females and help to bring them into reproductive condition. The vocalizations of owls may not echo musically through the woods like exquisite birdsong, but have precisely the same functions and are just as efficient.

BREEDING

Finding a mate can be a hazardous undertaking for an owl. As a territorial predator with powerful weapons, it is capable of defending its home against all comers. As males and females look the same as one another in almost all owl species, it is not easy to tell whether, at the start of the breeding season, an approaching bird is a member of the opposite sex seeking a mate or a rival of the same sex. Females are usually slightly bigger than males but this is not a good enough clue to establish the gender of another bird. More information is needed and this usually takes the form of differences in calls and in behaviour. Many owl species perform duets, with differing male and female calls being bounced back between one another. And the behaviour of an approaching female will also provide clues for a resident male. She will approach him in a manner that is appeasing and is neither too aggressive nor too frightened. Were she a rival male, the response to a male territory-owner would be either to fight or to flee. To appeal to a mate, the female must do neither of these things.

During the more intimate stages of owl courtship there is a great deal of beak-snapping, body swaying, bowing, wing raising, head waving and feather ruffling, as the pair attempt to achieve the synchronized arousal that will eventually lead to the mating act. Occasionally, food presentation (well known in other birds) has been observed in courting owls, when the male breaks off his displays to swoop down for a quick kill and then flies back up and offers the corpse to his female as a special gift.

The problems of choosing a partner are reduced by the fact that most owls are monogamous and therefore only face the difficult challenge of finding a suitable mate once in their lives. In many species the pair may not stay together during the non-breeding seasons of the year but even so, when the mating season arrives, they are only reacquainting themselves with one another, rather than starting from scratch.

For owls, finding a suitable nest-site is more important than building a nest. In terms of nest construction, owls are at the opposite end of the scale from weaver birds. Their nests are

Owl nest with young of different sizes.

typically clumsy, rough-and-ready affairs, but their selection of a nest-site is done with great care. They search for a protected cavity, a safe corner of a deserted or ruined building, a tree hollow, a rock crevice or the abandoned nest of some other bird. Once they have found a suitable site and made it their own, the female will lay a clutch of white, almost spherical eggs. She will usually do all the incubating herself during the 21–35 days it takes to hatch the eggs. Throughout this time her mate will bring food to the nest for her. Once the eggs have hatched, both parents will bring food for them. When the chicks are tiny the parents dismember the prey before passing it to them, making it easier for them to swallow.

The number of eggs varies enormously in different owls, but for most species three to four is the norm. The female usually allows several days between the laying of each egg, with the result that chicks are of different sizes. If food is plentiful all the chicks thrive but if it is scarce then only the larger chicks will survive. In bad times the younger chicks find it hard to compete for food and may starve to death in the nest, when they themselves

Threat display by a great horned owl (*Bubo virginianus*) – a flightless youngster in defensive posture.

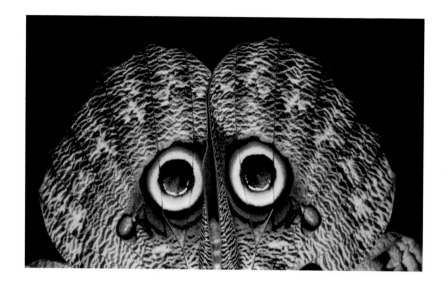

will become food for the older chicks. This harsh breeding system ensures that the parents produce the appropriate number of chicks for a particular environment.

Owl butterfly (*Caligo eurilochus sulanus*): a butterfly imitating an owl's face.

Owls may be poor nest-builders, but they are superb nest-defenders. If an intruder, including one as large as an adult human, comes too close to an occupied nest, the parent owl may either perform a dramatic defensive display or carry out a savage attack. The display consists of ruffling all the feathers, spreading the wings wide and then rotating them forwards and downwards. This has the effect of making the owl suddenly look enormous. In this threatening position it may proceed to clatter its beak and perform hissing and other sinister noises, as if saying, one step nearer and I will attack. Its huge, brightly coloured eyes stare fixedly at the intruder, adding further intimidation. The threatening quality of these eyes has led to the evolution of eye-spot display markings on the wings of some moths and butterflies that mimic the appearance of an owl's face. The most impressive example of this mimicry is found in the owl butterflies (genus *Caligo*).

An additional defence strategy of some owls is to perform a distraction display. This consists of a parent bird flapping around near the nest as if it is badly injured and therefore easy prey. In this way it tries to draw the attention of the intruder away from the helpless chicks in the nest. When the distracted intruder is about to pounce, the apparently vulnerable adult bird quickly flies away to safety and, with luck, the chicks will be overlooked.

On other occasions a full attack may be delivered in which the parent owl swoops low over the intruder's head and tries to slash it with its razor-sharp claws. One famous bird photographer, Eric Hosking, lost his left eye to a tawny owl in just such an encounter. He later published an autobiography with the sardonic title of *An Eye for a Bird*.

MOBBING

One of the strangest aspects of the natural history of owls is the treatment they receive from other birds. If an owl for some reason makes the mistake of appearing in the open during daylight hours it can expect to be quickly surrounded and attacked by a swarm of angry daytime birds. These may be considerably smaller than the owl but feel they have safety in numbers.

This mobbing behaviour has fascinated human observers since at least the sixth century BC. There is a beautiful Greek vase, a black-figure amphora, dating from that time, showing an owl tethered to a post underneath a tree. A flock of small birds fills the air around the captive owl and some of them have settled on the branches of the tree. These branches have been smeared with

Mobbing of tethered owl by the Bucci Painter (last quarter of 6th century BC), a Greek Attic black-figure amphora.

166

sticky bird-lime and, once they have landed there, the little birds are stuck fast and can easily be caught and killed for the pot. Even at this early date bird-catchers not only knew about the mobbing of owls but had learnt to exploit it.

Two centuries later, in his *Historia Animalium,* first published in 350 BC, Aristotle reveals that this knowledge had not been lost, when he writes: 'In the daytime all the other little birds flutter round the owl – a practice which is popularly termed "admiring him" – buffet him, and pluck out his feathers; in consequence of this habit, bird-catchers use the owl as a decoy for catching little birds of all kinds.'[3] The oddity in this comment is the use of the word 'admiring' for the act of mobbing. Because the Athenian owl was a revered symbol of wisdom, it was hard for a Greek author to view mobbing as the hatred of the owl by other birds. Instead it was more comfortable to suggest that 'it was the wisdom of the owl that the small birds wondered at.'

In Roman times Pliny mentions mobbing in his *Natural History* of AD 77–9. His description is a curious one but may have been based on an extreme case. He says: 'It is a pretty sight to see the wit and dexterity of these Howlets [little owls] when they fight with other birds: for when they are overlaid and beset with a multitude of them, they lie upon their backs and with their feet make shift to resist them: for gathering themselves into a narrow compass, there is nothing in a manner to be seen of them, save only their bill and talons, which cover the whole body.'[4]

The bestiaries of the thirteenth century often include a mobbed owl among their illustrations. There appears to have been a certain amount of cribbing from bestiary to bestiary, as the scene repeats itself with only minor variations. The owl is shown being pecked by three birds, the lower one being a magpie. The

Owl mobbed by
five birds, carved
on a misericord
at Norwich
Cathedral, East
Anglia, 1480.

immobile owl is seen suffering this indignity stoically, in a stiffly
upright posture. The pious bestiaries taught the lesson that the
owl was being attacked because, as a bird that courted darkness, it had 'rejected the light of Christ'.[5] And to make the bird
seem even more sinister one bestiary even claimed that the owl
flew backwards.

A little later, in the fifteenth century, five small birds are seen
attacking another long-suffering owl, this time carved in wood
on a misericord (the carved ledge below the seat) in Norwich
Cathedral. Similar carvings can be seen in a number of other
English churches of this period, from Yorkshire in the north
right down to Somerset near the south coast.

In the early sixteenth century Albrecht Dürer deserts his usually naturalistic style of rendering animals and gives us a desper-
ate, wild-eyed owl with feathers raised and wings flapping as it is
tormented by four angry birds, with their razor-sharp beaks and

Albrecht Dürer,
*Owl in Combat
with Day Birds,*
1509–15, woodcut.

claws ready to attack. The following century Francis Barlow
shows an owl mobbed at the entrance to its nest. His owl looks
bewildered and the seven birds attack from all sides. Barlow
describes his scene as symbolizing a sinner attacked by the righteous, feeling the need to give his picture a moral message despite
the fact that it is a reasonably realistic portrayal.

A much more naturalistic seventeenth-century treatment of
mobbing is to be found in a mosaic in Florence by Marcello
Provenzale (1575–1639), where the artist depicts an owl
harassed by a whole variety of precisely portrayed species,
including the robin, goldfinch, greenfinch, chaffinch, sparrow
and great tit. Ornithologically speaking, this mosaic is two centuries ahead of its time.

Moving on to the present, these works of art have largely been replaced by photographs snatched by bird-watchers who are lucky enough to come upon one of these avian dramas. Thanks to their observations we also have much more detailed descriptions of exactly what happens when a stranded owl becomes the victim of mob violence.

It is worth asking how the daytime birds develop this uncharacteristically bellicose habit. Small birds everywhere suffer from a lifelong fear of owls. It is an inborn fear that develops when they are only a few months old, regardless of whether they have ever met an owl. Confirming this is the fact that, as mentioned earlier, some moths and butterflies have evolved an owl-eye marking on their wings that they can flash at small birds approaching too closely and which frightens them away.

This inborn fear of owls generally results in a life-saving avoidance of these predatory birds, but occasionally – usually

Owl being mobbed: Marcello Provenzale's 17th-century mosaic, 'Landscape with Birds'.

when they have companions near them – the tormented become the tormentors. Instead of fleeing, they stand their ground and confront the owl. Screeching an alarm call, they attract more and more small birds to the scene until the bird of prey is surrounded by a noisy, angry mob. They now start to harass the bigger bird, calling incessantly and loudly, twisting and jerking their bodies and even making mock attacks. Sometimes a particularly bold individual will risk a real attack, swooping in from behind the owl and striking at its plumage.

This mobbing behaviour never occurs when the predator is actively hunting. It is most likely to occur when the owl is behaving in an odd way. If it is injured or sick it may sit quietly in an unusually visible position during daylight hours. A conspicuous stationary owl is a major target for mobbing. The small birds gather around and approach it remarkably closely, often as near as 3 metres (10 feet), and then start to display. The exact movements vary from species to species but in a typical finch such as the chaffinch the body is turned towards the owl, the crown-feathers are raised, the legs are bent, the wings are slightly raised, and the body is jerked quickly from side to side in a crouched posture, while the tail flicks up and down.

Many species have been seen to indulge in this strange mobbing display, including finches, tits, buntings, warblers, blackbirds, thrushes and even little hummingbirds. The hummingbirds become particularly hostile, buzzing around the big bird's head, as close as 5 cm (2 inches) from its face, calling out and jabbing at its eyes. Some of the larger birds, like the blackbirds and thrushes, often risk a little dive-bombing, in which they swoop down on the owl from 9 metres (30 feet), heading straight for it, and then swerve aside only at the very last moment, when they are no more than a foot away. Sometimes they leap at it from behind and claw at its head feathers.

A great horned owl mobbed by crows at Root River, Racine County, Wisconsin.

The excitement is contagious, with many new birds arriving and performing the mobbing display without even seeing the owl that is causing the commotion. They witness the behaviour of the other small mobbers and simply follow suit. They become so excited during this gang warfare that humans can approach them much more closely than at other times. And their arousal is so intense that if the owl finally departs they will still go on mobbing for a long time afterwards, as though they cannot calm down to a normal level of activity until some considerable time has passed.

The beleaguered owl gives the appearance of finding the whole encounter highly distasteful and confusing. Its bearing suggests that it is irritated and jarred by what is taking place around it. It becomes increasingly ill at ease until eventually the din and the intrusions become too much for it and it flaps off to find a quieter spot somewhere else. And this, of course, is the function of the combined display onslaught. The owl will not forget the ordeal and may in future avoid that particular district. For the local small birds this is a huge advantage.

The question remains as to how the small birds identify the owl. What are the special features that trigger such a powerful response? Field tests using stuffed owls and wooden dummies have established that the important features that make an owl an owl are: a big head, a short tail, solid contours, brown or grey colouring, a patterned surface with spots or streaks, a beak and frontally directed eyes. The more of these properties a dummy possesses the more strongly it is mobbed, but it seems to make little difference whether the object is a stuffed owl with real plumage or an owl-shaped piece of painted wood. If the key elements of owlness are absent, or only a few are present, the small birds show some curiosity about the dummy but are not stimulated to perform the full mobbing response.

One particular owl quality that is sufficient by itself to attract mobbing birds is the characteristic hooting sound it makes. This is a fact that was known all too well to plumage hunters in Trinidad, back in the days when hummingbird feathers were fashionable costume accessories. They discovered that simply by imitating the hooting of the local owls they could draw the unfortunate hummingbirds towards them and to their deaths.

CONSERVATION

After centuries of persecution, owls are at last being appreciated for the dramatically wonderful birds that they are. There are many excellent owl protection and conservation organizations, and careful studies have been made to assess the surviving populations of the different species. Of the approximately 200 species of owls alive today, conservationists have listed eleven as endangered and a further six as critically endangered (marked * on table overleaf). The species in serious trouble are shown overleaf.

The cause is always much the same – loss of habitat. Most owls need forests and forests are being decimated all over the world. For some species the long-term future looks bleak. The other threat is that pesticides are being widely employed to reduce the numbers of the kind of animals that owls need for their diet. And in a few backward regions there are still dark superstitions about owls that see them destroyed as evil spirits.

Public concern about endangered owls did, however, receive a boost from Hollywood in 2006 with the release of a feature film called HOOT. Described as an 'eco-thriller', the story is about a group of teenagers who take on Florida land developers whose bulldozers are threatening the habitat of the local burrowing

SPECIES	FORMAL NAME	POPULATION	CAUSE
Taliabu masked owl	*Tyto nigrobrunnea*	250–999 and decreasing	extensive logging
Madagascar red owl	*Tyto soumagnei*	1,000–2,499 and decreasing	destruction of habitat
Congo Bay owl	*Phodilus prigoginei*	2,500–9,999 and decreasing	forest clearance
Sokoke Scops owl	*Otus ireneae*	2,500 and decreasing	loss of nest-sites
Serendib Scops owl	*Otus thilohoffmanni*	250–999 and decreasing	habitat loss
Flores Scops owl	*Otus alfredi*	1,000–2,499 and decreasing	habitat loss
Siau Scops owl*	*Otus siaoensis*	less than 50	habitat destruction
Seychelles Scops owl	*Otus insularis*	249–318 and stable	small population
Biak Scops owl	*Otus beccarii*	500–9,999 and decreasing	fragmented habitat
Anjouan Scops owl*	*Otus capnodes*	50–249 and decreasing	habitat destruction
Moheli Scops owl*	*Otus moheliensis*	400 and decreasing	severely restricted habitat
Grand Comoro Scops owl*	*Otus pauliani*	2,000 and decreasing	severely restricted habitat
Blakiston's fish owl	*Ketupa blakistoni*	250–999 and decreasing dam	construction
Rufous fishing owl	*Scotopelia ussheri*	1,000–2,499 and decreasing	forest loss
Pernambuco pygmy owl*	*Glaucidium mooreorum*	less than 50 and decreasing	severely restricted habitat
Long-whiskered owlet	*Xenoglaux loweryi*	250–999 and decreasing	rapidly declining habitat
Forest owlet*	*Heteroglaux blewitti*	50–249 and decreasing	fragmented population

owls. The dramatic poster for the film shows the teenagers standing defiantly between an owl in its burrow and an approaching
bulldozer. The fact that the Hollywood film industry considers
such a plotline commercially viable is good news for the conservation of owls.

Another cause for celebration is that of the 200 species of
owls, over 180 are listed in the conservation category of 'Least

Concern'. Some of them have almost unassailable populations. The great horned owl, for example, has an estimated world population of no fewer than 5,300,000. And the barn owl almost matches it, with 4,900,000. The owls, with their special, nocturnal solution to the problem of survival, have always been a globally successful family of birds and with figures like these it would seem that they are here to stay.

10 Unusual Owls

As a whole the owls are a remarkably uniform group of birds. They may vary a little from species to species in their plumage colouring, their facial markings and their ear-tufts, but their way of life as nocturnal hunters seems to suit a rather rigid, basic owl design and aberrant species are a rarity. Despite this there are a few that do deserve special mention because they have strayed from this typical owl form in one direction or another. Some have become unusually large, some exceptionally small, and some have descended from the trees to inhabit underground burrows. Finally, a recently extinct owl was reputed to have lost the power of flight and has gained a rather strange legendary status.

THE GIANT OWL

The most dramatic owl in the world is the Eurasian eagle owl. Weighing 3,000 gm (6½ lb), with a body up to 72 cm (28 inches) long, and with a staggering wing-span of as much as 175 cm (69 inches) it is a giant among owls and a feared predator. Its diet includes the usual rodents but it also, surprisingly, hunts other owls. This is very much a one-way relationship – no other owl would ever dare to attack an eagle owl. It also preys upon diurnal birds of prey such as hawks, harriers, kites, buzzards, falcons

Eurasian eagle owl (*Bubo bubo*).

and even the occasional eagle. In fact its diet is enormously varied. In addition to birds of prey it has also been known to kill and eat ducks, coots, grebes, grouse, partridges, quail, doves, pigeons, gulls, waders, woodpeckers, crows, jackdaws, jays, magpies, nutcrackers, larks, thrushes, starlings, swifts, swallows, cormorant, herons, bitterns, bustards, cranes and even ravens. It is the same with mammals. In addition to rats, mice and voles it also devours rabbits, hares, deer fawns, chamois and ibex kids, wild sheep and their lambs, squirrels, stoats, weasels, mink, martens, foxes, bats, domestic cats, moles, shrews and hedgehogs. Clearly, nothing is safe when the great eagle owl is on the prowl and no owl in the world has such an impressively varied diet.

Most owls would be frightened of a large crowd of cheering, shouting people, but to one magnificent eagle owl they meant nothing. In 2007 a major international football match was taking place between Belgium and Finland in the national stadium in Helsinki. In the middle of the game the giant bird swooped down on the players and landed on the pitch. The referee stopped play and took the players off, to await the owl's departure. To his relief he saw the great bird spread its wings and fly up as if to bid farewell to the noisy crowd. Instead it settled majestically on the cross-bar of one of the goals, and rotated its head this way and that, taking in the human spectacle all around it. Seemingly puzzled rather than scared, it then took off again. The crowds cheers turned to laughter when, instead of fleeing the scene it settled itself on the goal at the other end of the stadium and proceeded to stare at the opposing football fans amassed there. Eventually it did depart and the game was resumed, but its lordly presence at the stadium revealed two things. First, the Eurasian eagle owl feared no man and, second, no man was brave enough to attempt to drive it away.

Since this incident, Finland's national football team has become known as the *Huuhkajat*, Finnish for Eurasian eagle owls, and the owl itself was named Helsinki Citizen of the Year in December 2007. It was given the name of Bubi and an investigation revealed that it was an urbanized owl. It had been using the A-stand of the arena as a regular roosting spot for some time and was obviously upset on this occasion to find its personal territory occupied by thousands of cheering football fans.

A more recent claim to fame is that the eagle owl is the species that appears as the family owl of the Malfoys in the Harry Potter stories by J. K. Rowling.

This is indeed the king of owls, and it seems somehow fitting that these great birds employ the ancient Step Pyramid at Saqqara as an annual breeding site. A sad footnote, however, is that this super-owl is falling prey to human persecution and its numbers are dwindling. Its fearless attitude to mankind has not helped it in this respect, and it seems to be unusually susceptible to collisions with road and rail traffic and especially to overhead wires and power lines.

THE SMALLEST OWL

The smallest owl in the world is the tiny elf owl that nests in large cacti in Mexico and the southern states of the USA. Weighing 40 gm (1$^1/_2$ oz) and with a body length of only 14 cm (5$^1/_2$ inches) it is not big enough to feast on small mammals or birds. Instead it enjoys a diet of large insects such as locusts, grasshoppers and crickets. It also eats beetles, moths, spiders, centipedes and the occasional scorpion. It takes large insects when they are settled on plants but is also capable of catching them in mid-air, either in its talons or in its beak. When living near to human habitation, the hunting elf owl is known to

exploit the swarms of night-flying insects that are attracted to outside electric lights.

Unusually for an owl, it does not have silent flight, presumably having no need for that degree of stealth when hunting its invertebrate prey. Another unusual feature is that it possesses only ten tail feathers, when all other owls have twelve. Vocally, it whimpers, whines, yips and barks like a young puppy. The males can be aggressive in defence of their nests but the females are more likely to feign death with closed eyes and an apparently lifeless body. During the day the elf owl employs a special hiding strategy, remaining immobile in an erect posture with its feathers pressed close to it body, one wing drawn forward, and its facial disc narrowed. In this way it mimics a broken branch or a stump of wood and avoids detection.

THE BURROWING OWL

The strange little burrowing owls, with their spindly legs, bright yellow eyes and an unusually vertical posture, are found throughout the whole length of the Americas from the short-grass prairies of Canada in the north, to the pampas of Argentina and Chile in the far south. In addition to these grasslands they are also encountered in desert and semi-desert regions and today even in human suburbs, including golf courses and airports.

The burrowing owl has several very un-owl-like features. Anatomically, its legs look more like those of a chicken than of an owl. A typical owl sits on a branch with only its feet showing, its legs mostly hidden by its lower plumage. The burrowing owl, spending nearly all its time either on the ground or below ground level, has unusually long legs, most of which are fully visible. Its behaviour is also very odd for a member of the owl family. Instead of nesting or roosting high above ground, safely out of the reach

Elf owl (*Microthene whitneyi*), the smallest owl, here nesting in cactus.

A burrowing owl at the entrance to a burrow.

of ground-dwelling predators, the burrowing owl, as its name suggests, makes its home in underground tunnels, sometimes dug by itself, but more often borrowed from the warrens of large rodents such as prairie dogs or viscachas.

The ground squirrels known as prairie dogs used to exist in vast numbers in the Americas before human populations began to proliferate and interfere with the long-established balance of nature. Even as late as the early twentieth century some colonies had populations of as many as a hundred million individuals. Their burrow systems, extending for miles in all directions, provided the perfect habitat for the little burrowing owls and they too flourished. When the rodents were exterminated as pests over huge areas of the continent the owl populations disappeared with them and today they are far less common than in previous centuries.

The social relations between the owls and the rodents are complicated. In some regions the two populations live side by side, more or less ignoring one another. In others there is considerable hostility. There is an old folk legend suggesting that the burrowing owls, rodents and rattlesnakes all live together in harmony and share the same burrows, but this is not the case. The owls drive out the rodents when they take over a burrow and the rattlesnakes are only there as predators.

Burrowing owls use their underground tunnels both for sleeping and for nesting. The nests are unusual, being lined with the dung of large grazing mammals. This is a refinement not found with typical owls and it aids the nestlings of the burrowing owl by masking their odour and effectively concealing them from scent-hunting predators. This is important because, being reared in underground tunnels, the nestlings are unusually vulnerable to nocturnal mammalian predators such as weasels, opossums and badgers. If the odour-masking fails to work and the predator comes close to the nest the young owls have one final strategy left with which to protect themselves. They have evolved a special alarm call that combines hissing noises and rattling sounds – mimicking a venomous rattlesnake. Weasels and other small carnivores will think twice about getting any closer in the dark of the tunnel and may then retreat. Of course, if the predator happens to be a rattlesnake this strategy fails.

Burrowing owls are active by day as well as at dawn and dusk and are the least nocturnal of all owls. They even hunt for lizards and large insects in the bright noonday sun. In keeping with their preference for living at a low level they sometimes chase their prey across the ground. In addition to animal foods, burrowing owls, uniquely among members of their family, also devour fruits and seeds. In some regions they favour cacti fruit such as those of the prickly pear.

Typical owls are never seen in colonies or large groups, and here again the burrowing owls are atypical, because they can often be observed roosting or nesting in groups of ten pairs or more. Several families may gather together outside their nesting burrows in regions where the populations are at a high level, making this a very unusual kind of owl indeed.

THE FLIGHTLESS OWL

One of the most mysterious of all owls is the extinct Bahaman great owl (*Tyto pollens*), known only from sub-fossils. Also referred to as the Andros Island barn owl or the Bahaman barn owl, this extinct species was a relative of today's common barn owl. A giant among owls it was said to stand 1 metre (39 inches) tall and to have lost the power of flight. It lived in the old pine forests of Andros Island, the largest of the Bahamas, and nested in burrows. It managed to survive the arrival of Europeans in the sixteenth century until they cut down its forests, when it quickly disappeared.

It gave rise to a local legend about a malicious bird-like dwarf with an owl-like face, glowing red eyes, a head that could rotate in any direction, three fingers, three toes and a tail that was used to hang from trees. The early settlers on the island told wild stories about this mischievous nocturnal imp, called a Chickcharnie, claiming that it built its nest by joining two pine trees together at the top. Anyone sightseeing on Andros is advised to carry flowers or bright bits of cloth to charm these troublesome beings, and not to molest them or sneer at them. If you respect them you will be blessed with good luck for the rest of your life, if not your head will turn completely around and you will suffer terrible misfortune. Having exterminated the real bird the locals now seem intent on protecting its ghost.

Bizarrely, the Chickcharnie is said to have been responsible for World War II. The story is told that, as a young man, Neville Chamberlain, who would later become the British prime minister, was chopping down trees on Andros Island to make way for a plantation when he came across a Chickcharnie nest, high in the pines. His local workmen refused to touch it and fled in terror, but he ignored their warnings and chopped down the trees himself, destroying the nest and bringing on himself a lifetime curse. It was this curse that led to his notorious failure at Munich which led to the outbreak of World War II. However one looks at it, this is quite an achievement for an extinct owl.

Timeline of the Owl

60 MYA	30,000 YEARS AGO		1898 BC

Fossil owls show that this branch of nocturnal bird predators has already begun

Oldest image of owl engraved on the roof of Chauvet Cave, France

Owls feature in the wall paintings of Twelfth Dynasty Egypt

1508	1797–9	1828	1850

Albrecht Dürer's famous drawing of a little owl

Goya's etching: *The Sleep of Reason Produces Monsters*

Audubon's *Birds of America* illustrates 14 species of owls

Florence Nightingale acquires a pet owl in Athens

1946	1950s	1960	

Picasso adopts an injured little owl in Antibes

Mick Southern undertakes a monumental study of the feeding ecology of owls

Eskimo artist Kenojuak creates her iconic *Enchanted Owl* stonecut

1200 BC	7TH CENTURY BC	400 BC TO AD 200	13TH CENTURY

Bronze owls appear in the art of the Shang dynasty in ancient China

Greek Proto-Corinthian perfume container in the form of an owl

Owls appear on ancient Greek coinage of Athens

Bestiary illustration showing an owl mobbed by birds

1867	1900	1920S	1939

The Owl and the Pussycat go to sea in Lear's Nonsense verse

Sheffield Wednesday Football Club becomes known as *The Owls*

A. A. Milne's Winnie-the-Pooh immortalizes WOL, a wise old owl

James Thurber introduces *The Owl who was God*

1962	2001	2005	2006

Roger Payne proves that owls, using only their ears, can locate their prey in complete darkness

Snowy owl Hedwig appears in the first Harry Potter film

Tracey Emin sees herself as an owl in her etching *Little Owl – Self-portrait*

Feature film *HOOT* released, showing attempts to defend owls against land developers

Appendix: Classification of Owls

One of the first attempts to classify owls scientifically is that of Pliny in AD77. In Book x of his *Natural History* he identifies three species of owls: the little owl, the eagle owl and the screech owl. By the sixteenth century Conrad Gesner (1560) had increased this number to four,[1] and by the seventeenth century, in the monumental 13-volume *Natural History* of Ulysses Aldrovandus, it had risen to eleven, all wonderfully illustrated in large woodcuts.[2] This marks the start of a serious, scientific attempt to organize and illustrate the owl species and to comment on their differences, but it was not until the nineteenth century that zoologists began to venture into the more obscure parts of the world to locate and collect the specimens that would soon fill the basements of the great natural history museums. During the twentieth century this process was energetically continued until it became increasingly difficult for even the most intrepid exploring scientist to locate a new large species of any animal. However, this does still occasionally happen and even within the last few years a new owl species has been discovered.

Today authorities vary considerably in their opinions concerning exactly how many species of owls there are. Some accept as few as 150, while others list as many as 220. One of the main reasons for this huge discrepancy is that many owls live on small islands where they develop slight differences from their close relatives on the nearby mainland. It then becomes a matter of taste as to whether you consider one of these isolated populations of owls as a distinct species or not. For example, there is a kind of barn owl that is found on the Andaman Islands in the Indian Ocean. It is significantly smaller than the mainland form, but

because the two never encounter one another in the wild it is impossible to tell whether, if they did meet, they would freely interbreed or remain completely separate. So one can only guess as to whether they are genuinely distinct species or not. If you happen to be an objective zoologist you are likely to lump the two together as races of the same species, but if instead you are a passionate conservationist you are more likely to view the island form as a distinct and therefore very rare species that needs urgent protection.

In an attempt to satisfy both schools of thought, the following classification aims to find a balance between the two extremes, accepting about 200 kinds of owls as genuine species. It is as up-to-date as possible and includes some species that were not even discovered until the twenty-first century.

Barn owl from Conrad Gesner, *Nomenclator Aquatilium Animantium* (1560).

Horned owl from Ulysses Aldrovandus, *Ornithologia*, Book VIII, from *Opera Omnia* (1656).

Order: Strigiformes (198 species)

FAMILY TYTONIDAE (15 SPECIES)

BARN OWLS

Sooty owl	*Tyto tenebricosa*	Australia, New Guinea
Sulawesi golden owl	*Tyto inexspectata*	Northern Sulawesi
Talaibu masked owl	*Tyto nigrobrunnea*	Sula Islands, Moluccas
Lesser masked owl	*Tyto sorocula*	Tanimbar Islands, Lesser Sundas
Manus masked owl	*Tyto manusi*	Manus Island, in Admiralty Islands
Bismarck masked owl	*Tyto aurantia*	New Britain
Australian masked owl	*Tyto novaehollandiae*	Australasia, New Guinea
Sulawesi owl	*Tyto rosenbergii*	Sulawesi (Celebes)
Madagascar red owl	*Tyto soumagnei*	Madagascar
Barn owl	*Tyto alba*	worldwide
Ashy-faced owl	*Tyto glaucops*	Haiti, Dominican Republic
African grass owl	*Tyto capensis*	Africa
Eastern grass owl	*Tyto longimembris*	South Asia, Australasia

BAY OWLS

Congo Bay owl	*Pholidus prigoginei*	Congo Basin, Africa
Oriental Bay owl	*Phodilus badius*	Asia

FAMILY STRIGIDAE (183 SPECIES)

SCREECH OWLS

Western screech owl	*Megascops kennicotti*	W. North America & Mexico
Balsas screech owl	*Megascops seductus*	Mexico
Pacific screech owl	*Megascops cooperi*	W. Central America
Eastern screech owl	*Megascops asio*	E. North America
Whiskered screech owl	*Megascops trichopsis*	Arizona & Central America
Tropical screech owl	*Megascops choliba*	Central & S. America
Koepcke's screech owl	*Megascops koepckeae*	Bolivia & Peru
West Peruvian screech owl	*Megascops roboratus*	Ecuador & Peru
Bare-shanked screech owl	*Megascops clarkii*	Costa Rica, Panama & Colombia
Bearded screech owl	*Megascops barbarus*	Guatemala & S. Mexico
Rufescent screech owl	*Megascops ingens*	Venezuela to Bolivia
Colombian screech owl	*Megascops colombianus*	Colombia & Ecuador
Cinnamon screech ow	*Megascops petersoni*	Ecuador & Peru

Cloud-forest screech owl	*Megascops marshalli*	Peru
Tawny-bellied screech owl	*Megascops watsonii*	Amazon Basin, S. America
Black-capped screech owl	*Megascops atricapillus*	E. South America
Vermiculated screech owl	*Megascops guatemalae*	Mexico to N.-W. Argentina
Montane Forest screech owl	*Megascops hoyi*	Argentina & Bolivia
Long-tufted screech owl	*Megascops sanctaecatarinae*	Argentina & Brazil
Puerto Rican screech owl	*Megascops nudipes*	Caribbean islands
White-throated screech owl	*Megascops albogularis*	N. Andes

SCOPS OWLS

White-fronted Scops owl	*Otus sagittarius*	S.-E. Asia
Rufous Scops owl	*Otus rufescens*	S.-E Asia
Sandy Scops owl	*Otus icterorhynchus*	W. Africa
Sokoke Scops owl	*Otus ireneae*	Kenya
Andaman Scops owl	*Otus balli*	Andaman Islands
Mountain Scops owl	*Otus spilocephalus*	Asia
Serendib Scops owl	*Otus thilohoffmanni*	Asia
Simeulue Scops owl	*Otus umbra*	Simeulue Islands, Sumatra
Javan Scops owl	*Otus angelinae*	Java
Sulawesi Scops owl	*Otus manadensis*	Sulawesi
Sangihe Scops owl	*Otus collari*	Sangihe Islands, Sulawesi
Luzon Scops owl	*Otus longicornis*	Luzon, Philippines
Mindoro Scops owl	*Otus mindorensis*	Mindoro, Philippines
Mindanao Scops owl	*Otus mirus*	Mindanao, Philippines
Sao Tomé Scops owl	*Otus hartlaubi*	Sao Tomé & Principe
Pallid Scops owl	*Otus brucei*	Middle East to Central Asia
Flammulated owl	*Otus flammeolus*	W. North America & Central America
Common Scops owl	*Otus scops*	Eurasia
African Scops owl	*Otus senegalensis*	Sub-Saharan Africa
Oriental Scops owl	*Otus sunia*	S. & E. Asia
Nicobar Scops owl	*Otus alius*	Nicobar Islands
Elegant Scops owl	*Otus elegans*	islands off S. Japan, Taiwan, Luzon
Mantanani Scops owl	*Otus mantananensis*	Philippines & Malaysia
Flores Scops owl	*Otus alfredi*	Flores Island
Siau Scops owl	*Otus siaoensis*	Siau Island, Sulawesi, Indonesia
Enggano Scops owl	*Otus enganensis*	Enggano Island, Sumatra
Seychelles Scops owl	*Otus insularis*	Mahé, Seychelles
Biak Scops owl	*Otus beccari*	Biak Island, Geelvink Bay, Papua
Madagascar Scops owl	*Otus rutilus*	Madagascar
Pemba Scops owl	*Otus pembaensis*	Pemba Island, off Tanzania

Anjouan Scops owl	*Otus capnodes*	Anjouan Island, Comoros, Indian Ocean
Torotoroka Scops owl	*Otus madagascariensis*	W Madagascar
Mayotte Scops owl	*Otus mayottensis*	Comoro Islands, Indian Ocean
Moheli Scops owl	*Otus moheliensis*	Mohéli Island, Comoros, Indian Ocean
Grand Comoro Scops owl	*Otus pauliani*	Grand Comoro, Indian Ocean
Rajah's Scops owl	*Otus brookii*	Sumatra, Java, Borneo
Collared Scops owl	*Otus bakkamoena*	S. & E. Asia, Indonesia & Japan
Mentawai Scops owl	*Otus mentawi*	Mentawai, W. Sumatra, Indonesia
Palawan Scops owl	*Otus fuliginosus*	Philippines
Whitehead's Scops owl	*Otus megalotis*	Luzon Islands, Philippines
Lesser Sunda Scops owl	*Otus silvicola*	Flores & Sumbawa, Sunda Islands
White-faced Scops owl	*Otus leucotis*	Sub-Saharan Africa
Palau Scops owl	*Otus podarginus*	Palau Islands

BARE-LEGGED OWL

| Bare-legged owl | *Gymnoglaux lawrencii* | Cuba |

GIANT SCOPS OWL

| Giant Scops owl | *Mimizuku gurneyi* | Philippines |

EAGLE OWLS

Snowy owl	*Bubo scandiaca*	Arctic
Great horned owl	*Bubo virginianus*	N. & S. America
Eurasian eagle owl	*Bubo bubo*	Europe & Asia
Rock eagle owl	*Bubo bengalensis*	S. Asia
Pharaoh eagle owl	*Bubo ascalaphus*	N. Africa & Middle East
Cape eagle owl	*Bubo capensis*	E. & S. Africa
Spotted eagle owl	*Bubo africanus*	Arabia & Sub-Saharan Africa
Fraser's eagle owl	*Bubo poensis*	W. Africa
Usambara eagle owl	*Bubo vosseleri*	Tanzania
Forest eagle owl	*Bubo nipalensis*	India & S.-E. Asia
Malay eagle owl	*Bubo sumatranus*	S. Asia
Shelley's eagle owl	*Bubo shellyei*	W. Africa
Verreaux's eagle owl	*Bubo lacteus*	Sub-Saharan Africa
Dusky eagle owl	*Bubo coromandus*	India & S.-E. Asia
Akun eagle owl	*Bubo leucostictus*	W. Africa
Philippine eagle owl	*Bubo philippensis*	Philippines

'Bubo maximus', from Saverio Manetti, *Ornithologia Methodice Digesta atque Iconibus Aeneis*, I (Florence, 1767).

'Athene noctua', from John Gould, *The Birds of Great Britain*, IV (1873).

Brown wood owl	*Strix leptogrammica*	India, S. China, S.-E. Asia
Tawny owl	*Strix aluco*	Europe, Asia, N. Africa, Middle East
Hume's tawny owl	*Strix butleri*	Middle East
Spotted owl	*Strix occidentalis*	W. North America & Mexico
Barred owl	*Strix varia*	North America & Mexico
Fulvus owl	*Strix fulvensis*	S. Mexico & N. Central America
Rusty-barred owl	*Strix hylophila*	Brazil, Uruguay & N.-E. Argentina
Rufous-legged owl	*Strix rufipes*	S. South America
Chaco owl	*Strix chacoensis*	Bolivia, Paraguay & Argentina
Ural owl	*Strix uralensis*	Central & N. Europe, Central Asia, Japan
David's wood owl	*Strix davidi*	China
Great grey owl	*Strix nebulosa*	N. Europe, Asia & N. America
African wood owl	*Strix woodfordii*	Sub-Saharan Africa
Mottled owl	*Strix virgata*	Mexico, Central & S. America
Black-and-white owl	*Strix nigrolineata*	Mexico to Ecuador
Black-banded owl	*Strix huhula*	N. & Central South America
Rufous-banded owl	*Strix albitarsus*	N. Andes

MANED OWL

| Maned owl | *Jubula letti* | W. Africa |

CRESTED OWL

| Crested owl | *Lophostrix cristata* | Central & N. South America |

SPECTACLED OWLS

Spectacled owl	*Pulsatrix perspicillata*	Mexico, Central & S. America
Band-bellied owl	*Pulsatrix melanota*	N. Andes
Tawny-browed owl	*Pulsatrix koeniswaldiana*	E. South America

HAWK OWL

| Hawk owl | *Surnia ulula* | N. North America, N. Europe, N. Asia |

PYGMY OWLS

Eurasian pygmy owl	*Glaucidium passerinum*	N. & Central Europe, N. Asia
Collared pygmy owl	*Glaucidium brodiei*	Himalayas, China & S.-E. Asia
Pearl-spotted owlet	*Glaucidium perlatum*	Sub-Saharan Africa
Northern pygmy owl	*Glaucidium gnoma*	W. North & Central America
Andean pygmy owl	*Glaucidium jardinii*	Central and N. South America
Costa Rican pygmy owl	*Glaucidium costaricanum*	Costa Rica & Panama
Cloud-forest pygmy owl	*Glaucidium nubicola*	Colombia & Ecuador

Yungas pygmy owl	*Glaucidium bolivianum*	Argentina, Bolivia & Peru
Pernambuco pygmy owl	*Glaucidium morreorum*	Brazil
Amazonian pygmy owl	*Glaucidium hardyi*	N. South America
Least pygmy owl	*Glaucidium minutissimum*	Mexico, Central & N. America
Central American pygmy owl	*Glaucidium griseiceps*	Central, S. & North America
Tamaulipas pygmy owl	*Glaucidium sanchezi*	Mexico
Colima pygmy owl	*Glaucidium palmarum*	Mexico
Subtropical pygmy owl	*Glaucidium parkeri*	Bolivia, Ecuador, Peru
Ferruginous pygmy owl	*Glaucidium brasilianum*	Central and S. America
Peruvian pygmy owl	*Glaucidium peruanum*	Ecuador & Peru
Austral pygmy owl	*Glaucidium nanum*	Argentina & Chile
Cuban pygmy owl	*Glaucidium siju*	Cuba
Red-chested owlet	*Glaucidium tephronotum*	Tropical Africa
Sjostedt's pygmy owl	*Glaucidium sjostedti*	W. Central Africa
Cuckoo owlet	*Glaucidium cuculoides*	China & S.-E. Asia
Javan owlet	*Glaucidium castanopterum*	Indonesia
Jungle owlet	*Glaucidium radiatum*	Pakistan to Burma
Chestnut-backed owlet	*Glaucidium castanotum*	Sri Lanka
Chestnut owlet	*Glaucidium castaneum*	Tropical W. Africa
African barred owlet	*Glaucidium capense*	Sub-Saharan Africa
Albertine owlet	*Glaucidium albertinum*	E. Zaire & Rwanda

'Nyctea nivea', from John Gould, *The Birds of Great Britain*, IV (1873).

'Assiolo asio', from Manetti's *Ornithologia*, I (1767).

LONG-WHISKERED OWL

Long-whiskered owl	*Xenoglaux loweryi*	N. Peru

ELF OWL

Elf owl	*Micrathene whitneyi*	S.-W. USA & Mexico

LITTLE OWLS

Little owl	*Athene noctua*	Europe, N. Africa, Middle East, Asia
Spotted little owl	*Athene brama*	S. Asia
Burrowing owl	*Athene cunicularia*	the Americas

FOREST SPOTTED OWL

Forest spotted owl	*Heteroglaux blewitti*	Central India

FOREST OWLS

Tengmalm's owl	*Aegolius funereu*	Europe, N. Asia, N. America
Northern saw-whet owl	*Aegolius acadicus*	N. America & N. Mexico
Unspotted saw-whet owl	*Aegolius ridgwayi*	S. Mexico & Central America
Buff-fronted owl	*Aegolius harrisii*	N.-W. & S. Central South America

HAWK OWLS

Rufous owl	*Ninox rufa*	N. Australia & New Guinea
Powerful owl	*Ninox strenua*	S.-E. Australia
Barking owl	*Ninox connivens*	Australia, New Guinea & Moluccas
Sumba boobook	*Ninox rudolfi*	Indonesia
Southern boobook	*Ninox novaeseelandiae*	Australasia
Little Sumba hawk owl	*Ninox sumbaensis*	Sumba, Indonesia
Brown hawk owl	*Ninox scutuluta*	S. & E. Asia
Andaman hawk owl	*Ninox affinis*	Andaman & Nicobar Islands
White-browed hawk owl	*Ninox superciliaris*	Madagascar
Philippine hawk owl	*Ninox philippensis*	Philippines
Cinnabar hawk owl	*Ninox ios*	Sulawesi (Celebes)
Ochre-bellied hawk owl	*Ninox ochracea*	Sulawesi (Celebes)
Togian hawk owl	*Ninox burhani*	Togian Islands, Sulawesi (Celebes)
Indonesian hawk owl	*Ninox squamipila*	S.-E. Asian islands
Christmas hawk owl	*Ninox natalis*	Christmas Island
Jungle hawk owl	*Ninox theomacha*	New Guinea
Admiralty Islands hawk owl	*Ninox meeki*	Admiralty Islands
Speckled hawk owl	*Ninox punctulata*	Sulawesi (Celebes)
Bismarck hawk owl	*Ninox variegata*	New Britain & New Ireland

New Britain hawk owl	*Ninox odiosa*	New Britain	'Noctua vulgaris', from Manetti's *Ornithologia*, I (1767).
Solomon Islands hawk owl	*Ninox jacquinoti*	Solomon Islands	

PAPUAN HAWK OWL

Papuan hawk owl	*Uroglaux dimorpha*	New Guinea	'Aluco aldrov', from Manetti's *Ornithologia*, I (1767).

PSEUDO-SCOPS OWLS

Jamaican owl	*Pseudoscops grammicus*	Jamaica
Striped owl	*Pseudoscops clamator*	Mexico, Central & S. America

FEARFUL OWL

Fearful owl	*Nesasio solomonensis*	Solomon Islands

EARED OWLS

Stygian owl	*Asio stygus*	Mexico, Central & S. America
Long-eared owl	*Asio otus*	Europe, Middle East, Asia, Africa
Abyssinian long-eared owl	*Asio abyssinicus*	E. Africa & Zaire
Madagascar long-eared owl	*Asio madagascariensis*	E. Madagascar
Short-eared owl	*Asio flammeus*	Europe, Asia & the Americas
African marsh owl	*Asio capensis*	Sub-Saharan Africa

References

1 PREHISTORIC OWLS

1 Jean-Marie Chauvet et al., *Chauvet Cave: The Discovery of the World's Oldest Paintings* (London, 1996), pp. 48–9.
2 Abbé H. Breuil, *Four Hundred Centuries of Cave Art* (Montignac, Dordogne, 1952), pp. 159 and 162, fig. 123.
3 Ann and Gale Sieveking, *The Caves of France and Northern Spain* (London, 1962), p. 188.
4 Rosemary Powers and Christopher B. Stringer, 'Palaeolithic Cave Art Fauna', *Studies in Speleology*, II / 7–8 (November 1975), pp. 272–3.

2 ANCIENT OWLS

1 Edward Terrace, *Egyptian Paintings of the Middle Kingdom* (London, 1968), p. 26.
2 Faith Medlin, *Centuries of Owls* (Norwalk, CT, 1967) p. 16.
3 Virginia C. Holmgren, *Owls in Folklore and Natural History* (Santa Barbara, CA, 1988), p. 31.
4 Edward A. Armstrong, *The Folklore of Birds* (London, 1958), p. 119.
5 C. Plinius Secundus, *The Historie of the World. Commonly called The Naturall Historie* (London, 1635), Tome I, Bk X, pp. 276–7.
6 Robert W. Bagley, *Shang Ritual Bronzes* (Cambridge, MA, 1987), pp. 114–16, figs 152–6.
7 Elizabeth P. Benson, *The Mochica: A Culture of Peru* (London, 1972) p. 52.

3 MEDICINAL OWLS

1 John Swan, *Speculum Mundi* (Cambridge, 1643), p. 397.

4 SYMBOLIC OWLS

1 Richard Barber, *Bestiary* (Woodbridge, Suffolk, 1993), p. 149.
2 Sir Walter Scott, *A Legend of Montrose* (London, 1819), chap. 6.
3 George Wither, *A Collection of Emblemes, Ancient and Moderne* (London, 1635), Bk 4, illus. XLV, p. 253.
4 Faith Medlin, *Centuries of Owls* (Norwalk, CT, 1967), p. 46.
5 E. L. Sambourne, *Punch* (10 April 1875).

5 EMBLEMATIC OWLS

1 Andrea Alciati, *Emblematum Liber* (Augsberg, 1531). This, the first book of emblems, was immensely popular and ran to 150 editions, the last version appearing in the eighteenth century (Madrid, 1749). A new edition with English translations by John F. Moffitt appeared in 2004, using illustrations from the 1549 edition.
2 Guillaume de la Perrière, *Morosophie* (Lyons, 1553), printed by Macé Bonhomme.
3 Georgette de Montenay, *Emblematum Christianorum centuria* (1584).
4 George Wither, *A Collection of Emblemes, Ancient and Moderne* (London, 1635), Bk 1, illus. IX, p. 9.
5 Ibid., Bk 2, illus. I, p. 63.
6 Ibid., Bk 2, illus. XVII, p. 79.
7 Ibid., Bk 3, illus. XXXIV, p. 168.

6 LITERARY OWLS

1 Lady Parthenope Verney, *Life and Death of Athena, an Owlet from the Parthenon* (privately printed, 1855). Later reissued as *Florence*

Nightingale's Pet Owl, Athena: A Sentimental History (San Francisco, 1970) in honour of the 150th anniversary of the birth of Florence Nightingale.

2 Lewis Carroll, *Alice's Adventures in Wonderland* (London, 1965), illus. to chap. 3.

7 TRIBAL OWLS

1 Norman Bancroft-Hunt, *People of the Totem: The Indians of the Pacific Northwest* (London, 1979), p. 97.

2 Jean Blodgett, *Kenojuak* (Toronto, 1985).

3 W. T. Larmour, *The Art of the Canadian Eskimo* (Ottawa, 1967), p. 16.

8 OWLS AND ARTISTS

1 Jacques Combe, *Jheronimus Bosch* (London, 1946), p. 10.

2 *Ibid.*, p. 21.

3 Wilhelm Fraenger, *Hieronymus Bosch* (Amsterdam, 1999), p. 201.

4 Mario Bussagli, *Bosch* (New York, 1967), p. 10.

5 Fraenger, *Hieronymus Bosch*, p. 44.

6 Herbert Read, *Hieronymus Bosch* (London, 1967), p. 5.

7 Fraenger, *Hieronymus Bosch*, p. 116.

8 Colin Eisler, *Dürer's Animals* (Washington, DC, 1991), pp. 83–5.

9 Mario Salmi et al., *The Complete Works of Michelangelo* (London, 1966), fig. 91, p. 119.

10 Philip Hofer, *The Disasters of War by Francisco Goya* (New York, 1967), a reproduction in its entirety of the first edition of Goya's *Los Desastres de la Guerra* (1863) published by the Real Academia de Nobles Artes de San Fernando. Plate 73: *Gatesca pantomima*.

11 Vivien Noakes, *Edward Lear, 1818–1888* (London, 1985), plate 10g, pp. 27 and 86.

12 David Duncan Douglas, *Viva Picasso* (New York, 1980), pp. 86–7.

13 Gertje R. Utley, *Picasso: The Communist Years* (New Haven, CT, 2000), p. 160, fig. 130.

14 Evelyn Benesch et al., *René Magritte: The Key to Dreams* (Vienna, 2005), p. 168.

15 David Sylvester, *René Magritte, Catalogue Raisonné* (London, 1993), vol. II, p. 340.

16 Silvano Levy, personal communication, 29 October 2008.

17 Dorothy C. Miller, *Americans, 1942* (New York, 1942), p. 56.

18 Krystyna Weinstein, *The Owl in Art, Myth, and Legend* (London, 1985), p. 59.

9 TYPICAL OWLS

1 Gordon Lynn Walls, *The Vertebrate Eye* (New York, 1967), p. 212.

2 Pellets are available from pelletsinc.com or pellet.com or pellet-lab.com in Washington State; owlpellets.com in California; owlpelletkits.com in New York State.

3 Aristotle, *Historia Animalium*, trans. D'Arcy Wentworth Thompson (Oxford, 1910), vol. IV, p. 609.

4 C. Pliny Secundus, *The Naturall Historie* (London, 1635), Tome I, Bk 10, ch. XVII, p. 277.

5 Ann Payne, *Medieval Beasts* (London, 1990), p. 73.

APPENDIX

1 Conrad Gesner, *Icones Avium* (Zürich, 1560), pp. 14–17.

2 Ulyssis Aldrovandi, *Opera Omnia* (Bologna, 1638–68), Libri XII, *Ornithologiae* (1646) pp. 498–570.

Bibliography

Armstrong, Edward, *The Life and Lore of the Bird* (New York, 1975)
——, *The Folklore of Birds* (London, 1958)
Backhouse, Frances, *Owls of North America* (Richmond Hill, ON, 2008)
Berger, Cynthia, *Owls* (Mechanicsburg, PA, 2005)
Breese, Dilys, *Everything You Wanted to Know About Owls* (London, 1998)
Bunn, D. S. *et al.*, *The Barn Owl* (Calton, Staffs, 1982)
Burton, J. A., *Owls of the World* (London, 1984)
Cenzato, Elena and Fabio Santopietro, *Owls: Art, Legend, History* (New York, 1991)
Clair, Colin, *Unnatural History* (New York, 1967)
Everett, M. J., *A Natural History of Owls* (London, 1977)
Grossman, Mary Louise and John Hamlet, *Birds of Prey of the World* (London, 1965)
Gruson, Edward S., *A Checklist of the Birds of the World* (London, 1976)
Holmgren, Virginia C., *Owls in Folklore and Natural History* (Santa Barbara, CA, 1988)
Hume, Rob, *Owls of the World* (Limpsfield, Surrey, 1991)
Johnsgard, P. A., *North American Owls – Biology and Natural History* (Washington, DC, 1988)
Kemp, A. and S. Calburn, *The Owls of Southern Africa* (Cape Town, 1987)
Konig, Claus and Friedhelm Weick, *Owls of the World* (London, 2008)
Konig, Claus, Friedhelm Weick and J.-H. Becking, *Owls: A Guide to the Owls of the World* (New Haven, CT, 1999)
Long, Kim, *Owls, a Wildlife Handbook* (Boulder, CO, 1998)

Lynch, Wayne, *Owls of the United States and Canada* (Baltimore, MD, 2007)

Medlin, Faith, *Centuries of Owls in Art and the Written Word* (Norwalk, CT, 1968)

Mikkola, Heimo, *Owls of Europe* (London, 1983)

Peeters, Hans, *A Field Guide to Owls of California and the West* (Berkeley, CA, 2007)

Scholz, Floyd, *Owls* (Mechanicsurg, PA, 2001)

Shawyer, Colin, *The Barn Owl* (London, 1994)

——, *The Barn Owl in the British Isles: Its Past, Present and Future* (London, 1987)

Sparks, John and Tony Soper, *Owls: Their Natural and Unnatural History* (New York, 1970)

Taylor, Iain, *Barn Owls* (Cambridge, 2004)

Voous, Karel H., *Owls of the Northern Hemisphere* (London, 1988)

Weick, Friedhelm, *Owls Strigiformes: Annotated and Illustrated Checklist* (Berlin, 2006)

Weinstein, Krystyna, *The Owl in Art, Myth, and Legend* (London, 1990)

Associations and Websites

THE AUSTRIAN BARN OWL PROJECT
www.schleiereule.at/english/englframe.html
A project to protect the barn owl in Austria.

BANGALORE BARN OWL CONSERVATION GROUP
www.bangalorebarnowl.com/barnowl.php

THE BARN OWL CENTRE OF GLOUCESTERSHIRE
www.barnowl.co.uk/
The centre helps provide a sanctuary for owls in need.

BOCN – THE BARN OWL CONSERVATION NETWORK
www.bocn.org/
A UK network of specialist voluntary advisors, working to help this species by promoting a nationwide habitat creation scheme.

THE BARN OWL CONSERVATION TRUST
www.barnowl.co.uk/

THE BARN OWL TRUST
www.barnowltrust.org.uk/
The Trust is at the centre of Barn Owl conservation in the UK.

BURROWING OWL CONSERVATION SOCIETY OF BC:
http://burrowingowlbc.org/
Based in British Columbia, Canada.

BURROWING OWL PRESERVATION SOCIETY:
Based in California.

COTSWOLD OWL RESCUE TRUST
www.owlrescue.supanet.com/
A conservation project to ensure a healthy gene pool.

HEREFORD OWL RESCUE
www.herefordowlrescue.co.uk/
A centre that looks after any owl that is in danger or unwanted.

THE HUNGRY OWL PROJECT
www.hungryowl.org/
Started in 2002, The Hungry Owl Project (HOP) is based in Marin
County, California. Its mission is to reduce the need for harmful
pesticides by encouraging natural predators and by providing a
resource of help and information on alternative methods of
sustainable pest management.

INTERNATIONAL OWL SOCIETY
www.international-owl-society.com/
Provides a worldwide forum for all those interested in owls.

THE OWL FOUNDATION
www.theowlfoundation.ca/
A conservation organization that operates a centre for the rehabili-
tation of Canadian Owl species, and the behavioural observation of
permanently damaged wild owls in a breeding environment.

OWL HALL OF FAME
www.globalowlproject.com/
The Global Owl Project (GLOW) proposes a multi-year, worldwide project to resolve aspects of taxonomy and conservation
for the world's owls.

THE OWL PAGES
www.owlpages.com/
An Australian website that disseminates information on all aspects of
owls.

OWL RESCUE
www.owlrescue.co.uk/
A one-stop source of information on the subject of owls.

WILD OWL
www.wildowl.co.uk/
Owl conservation project started in the spring of 2006.

WORLD OF OWLS
www.worldofowls.com/
A Northern Ireland centre working to ensure the survival of owls
throughout the world.

WORLD OWL TRUST
www.owls.org/ and www.worldowltrust.org/
Leading the world in owl conservation, a trust whose primary aim is
to ensure the survival of all species of the world's owls, promoting
scientific research, habitat creation and restoration. Headquarters:
World Owl Centre, Muncaster Castle, Ravenglass, Cumbria CA18 1RQ:
www.muncaster.co.uk/world-owl-centre

Photo Acknowledgements

The author and publishers wish to express their thanks to the below sources of illustrative material and/or permission to reproduce it. (Some information not placed in the captions for reasons of brevity is also given below.)

Illustration © ADAGP, Paris and DACS, London 2009: p. 132; from Eleazar Albin, *Natural History of Birds* (London, 1731): p. 6; from Andrea Alciati, *Emblemata* (Paris, 1584): p. 61; from Ulysses Aldrovandus, *Ornothologia*, Book VIII, from *Opera Omnia* (Bologna, 1656): pp. 149, 153, 191 (right); photo © Arte & Immagini srl/CORBIS: p. 171; photo Yann Arthus-Bertrand /Ardea.com: p. 155; author's collection: pp. 8, 22 (foot), 24, 30, 46, 50, 58, 65, 66, 67, 68, 71, 94, 95, 101, 103, 104, 105, 106, 107, 110 (FOOT), 135, 149, 153, 191; photo J. Bain: p. 57; photo © NCBateman1/BigStockPhoto: p. 159; photo Elizabeth Bomford/Ardea.com: p. 156; British Museum, London (photos © Trustees of the British Museum): pp. 19, 40; reproduced by permission of the artist (Claudia at Frith Street Tattoo, London) and Linsay Trerise: p. 110 (top); photo Tom Cooker: p. 146 (foot); photo Jerry DeBoer: p. 172; photo Mike Debreceni: p. 184; photo David Duncan Douglas: p. 127; photo Thomas Dressler/Ardea.com: p. 142; reproduced by kind permission of the artist (Tom Duimstra): p. 135; reproduced by kind permission of the Edmonton Summer Universiade Committee: p. 72; photo Jonker Fourie: p. 136; Galleria Delvecchio, Toronto: p. 33 (top right); by kind permission of Girlguiding UK: p. 69; photos courtesy Glasgow University Library (Department of Special Collections): pp. 61, 62, 63; from John Gould, *The Birds of Great Britain*, vol. IV (London, 1873): pp. 195 (right), 197 (left), Graphisches Sammlung Albertina, Vienna: p. 118; photos Doak Heyser: p. 32; photo © Holger Hollemann/epa/Corbis: p. 146 (top); photo John and Karen Hollingsworth/US Fish and Wildlife Service: p. 142; photo © Hulton-Deutsch Collection/CORBIS: p. 47; photo © karmaamarande/BigStock-Photo: p. 163; photo Albert W. Kerr: p. 169; reproduced by kind permission

Index